SENIOR CHOICES
REMARRIAGE OR RELATIONSHIPS

The Pleasures and Problems of
Romantic Encounters Over Sixty

SENIOR CHOICES
REMARRIAGE OR RELATIONSHIPS

The Pleasures and Problems of
Romantic Encounters Over Sixty

by

**Peggy Andrews Burns and
Willard A. Burns, M.D.**

ISBN: 1-58820-003-5

1stBooks - rev. 9/14/00

ABOUT THE BOOK

Men and women living together outside of marriage is common place today. But did you know that almost 400,000 seniors are part of this group. A new book, *Senior Choices----Remarriage or Relationships* by Dr. Willard Burns and his wife, Peggy Burns, explains this new trend and the choices seniors are making in light of longer, healthier life spans, more money to spend and the independence to enjoy it.

This new book, which acknowledges that marriage is still the most accepted lifestyle for two seniors, explores the alternatives. In doing so, it breaks down senior relationships according to the main characteristics that bring the couple together. It describes the "geriatric stud" as well as what the authors call a "comfort companionship".

Relationships are different at 60 plus because seniors are different than they were forty years earlier. They may be wiser but are usually more practical, sometimes more frugal, set in their ways, more prone to aches and pains and often in need of a nap. Any or all these characteristics may determine what type of relationship a senior may become involved in.

The authors discuss many problems facing unmarried couples that are different from those that chose marriage. According to the authors, money and children are the two biggest factors preventing remarriage but there are other stumbling blocks too. Legal problems and deteriorating health, both physical and mental, are discussed in the context of relationships starting after the age of 60. With senior moments, cracking joints and over active bladder problems, it's not easy to start a new relationship.

Is sex always a part of a new relationship? This book addresses seniors involved in sex and some of the misconceptions about their sexuality. It deals with the fears, expectations, consequences as well as the pleasures of sex at this age.

The serious subject of death and burial is also mentioned. A few suggestions are given with emphasis on the fact that unmarried couples may have little to say about their partner's burial site.

The book adds humor to the eccentricities of seniors in their everyday lives. For those seeking a new partner, it ends with a lengthy list of good dating tips.

DEDICATION

This book is dedicated to the children of
our new family and their families

Andy, Chris, Rick, Jeff
Wil, Clem and Mary

TABLE OF CONTENTS

INTRODUCTION

Men and women living together outside of marriage is common place today. But did you know that almost 400,000 seniors are part of this group? Our book explains this new trend and the choices' seniors are making in light of longer, healthier life spans, more money to spend and the independence to enjoy it.

Our children have taught us that relationships without marriage are OK. Because many young people feel it's an accepted way to live, future generations of seniors will probably not marry as often as they do today. We acknowledge that marriage is still the most accepted lifestyle for two seniors, but this book explores the alternatives. Our emphasis is on non-married couples who are available for a legal commitment but for various reasons chose not to marry.

In dealing with this new trend, we will discuss what a relationship is, types of relationships and various aspects that influence the direction and often the longevity of the partnership. In doing so, we will break down senior relationships according to the main characteristics that bring the couple together. We will describe the "geriatric stud" as well as what we call a "comfort companionship". The latter is undoubtedly the starting point of most partnerships and easily the most common relationship.

Relationships are different at 60 plus because seniors are different from what they were forty years earlier. They may be wiser but are usually more practical, sometimes more frugal, set in their ways, more prone to aches and pains and often in need of a nap. Any or all these characteristics may determine what type of relationship a senior may become involved in.

There are many problems facing unmarried couples that are different from those that choose marriage. Money and children seem to be the two biggest factors preventing remarriage but there are other stumbling blocks too. Just getting married doesn't solve all the problems. Legal problems and deteriorating health, both physical and mental, are discussed in the context of relationships starting after the age of 60. With senior moments, cracking joints and over active bladder problems, it's not easy to start a new relationship. Our commonsense approach to these problems may sound simplistic and generic at times but it is the reality of senior living. Our desire is to encourage seniors to enjoy the pleasures of later life but to be aware of the problems.

Is sex always a part of a new relationship? We address seniors involved in sex and some of the misconceptions about their sexuality. We deal with the fears, expectations, consequences as well as the pleasures of sex at this age.

The serious subject of death and burial is also mentioned. A few suggestions are given with emphasis on the fact that unmarried couples may have little to say about their partner's burial site.

This book adds humor to the eccentricities of seniors in their everyday lives. Our last chapter contains an abbreviated list of "dating tips" for active seniors that we believe are more appropriate for our age group than the rules of the younger generation. *For unattached singles, start with the last chapter! Enjoy!*

Chapter 1

Relationships After Sixty

Seniors today are living longer and for the most part are healthier than their parents and grandparents. Because of the death of a spouse or divorce, seniors are often left without a partner. There are many pleasures associated with romantic encounters over the age of sixty. Since social life is important, new relationships are constantly being formed. The social part of being in a relationship, even a fleeting one, makes it easier to participate in events in new surroundings. Other benefits of being part of a relationship are the sharing and growing in our later years with another individual. This new friend can help in time of need, giving support when family is not close and old friends may be ill or have passed away. A partner is easily available for all activities including those in the bedroom. Dancing, sports, bridge and travel are much more enjoyable and easier to do with a "significant other". The incentive to do ones' best, look ones' best, and act ones' best can be inspired by the expectations of another. A couple is more likely to be socially involved with other heterosexual couples than a solitary individual. Those alone are often involved with a same sex group. In addition, couples, with two incomes, are better able to manage the costs of many activities, including expensive travel.

Probably the most important aspect and one of the biggest pleasures of becoming involved in a relationship is the easing of loneliness. All seniors without a partner experience loneliness sometimes or always. This is particularly true for those who have lost their spouse to death or divorce in their later years.

It's one thing to have a relationship when you're young because it is often based on lust or luck. We're set in our ways and we bring the baggage of our upbringing with us. We try desperately to update ourselves but we're usually not totally successful. Most seniors don't want a purely sexual relationship. We want loving, caring and sharing to predominate. We also want someone that we can do things with and that we can depend upon. We don't want lots of talk about past doings but someone who thinks and wants to do things now with a mate. It's fun to date and have some good times but we want more. Even though older women have learned to invest money, repair leaking toilets and mow the lawn -- women want more than that. Not just women, we all want love, companionship and possibly, some sex too!

But finding the right one and making a commitment (whether legal or verbal) can be frightening. We never thought about adjustments in our 20's but now it's different. Life may only give us a quarter of the years we had with our previous partner so a new relationship requires more thought. In the "old" days, couples worried mostly about religious and parental approval. At this age, there seems to be a lot more to consider. Money, possessions, children and health are much more important now than before. We never worried about health in our twenties.

So, what is a relationship? Webster defines a relationship as kinship or an affinity or a state of affairs existing between those having relations or dealings. This really doesn't help us to define a relationship between two unrelated people as the term is currently used. An updated interpretation would define a relationship as a bonding of a couple, whether legal or verbal, sexual or not, in a social context. We will restrict our discussions to heterosexual couples over sixty years old.

Are all relationships the same for those over sixty?

No, they are not! Everyone is involved in constant relationships from the time that they are born. Our first relationship is with our parents and family. From there we branch out to school, work and friends trying to make more selective choices when opportunities come. As we grow older and hopefully wiser, choices are often diminished and out of our control. However, the seniors today are better off than they were fifty years ago. They have far more independence, better health, and more money to spend.

We have given several senior relationships titles. There may be other ways of categorizing and describing them but for reference we have chosen these names. We are sure that there are many more groups as well as types that we could describe but these we think are the most important.

The Comfort Relationship

The most rewarding and frequent type of heterosexual connection is best described as a *Comfort Relationship* which is a companionship comfortable for both. Both parties discover mutual interests and they are intellectually and socially very compatible. They fill a void in each other's life but respect the differences that each one has developed over the years. Most importantly, *they are comfortable* in each other's company, share common interests and enthusiastically become involved in activities as a couple. Whether couples in a comfort relationship become sexually involved, marry or not, they provide security, support and help to each other. Above all, they establish a confiding companionship for the ups and downs of everyday life. Any type of permanent partnership always begins with a comfort relationship.

Couples, not involved sexually with each other, can establish a comfortable friendship. The relationship would be similar to that of brother and sister, cousins or any close family members. These are very special associations that can exist over many years. They may have begun as early as grammar school and can often be renewed after many years of separation. They might have started in school, on the job, in the neighborhood or at clubs. This friendship is supportive in nature and is often well accepted by family and other friends. A sexual relationship with another party can go on simultaneously and does not interfere with this friendship.

Males and females can be partners in golf and tennis or play bridge together without any sexual undertones being present. Particularly for the single female, this is a way she may participate in social activities that call for mixed couples. It is also a pleasant method of companionship for both parties without the usual commitments of a couple. They will often travel together and share the same room without sex being part of the package. This is being done for both companionship on a trip and for economic reasons. Many tours prefer couples to singles as it's easier for them to make accommodations and they are not concerned whether couples are married or not. This is contrary to 40 years ago when hotels frowned on non-married couples and the male would sign as "Mr. and Mrs." even if they weren't. The majority of senior relationships are of the comfort type. As the number of active seniors increases, a variety of situations creating relationships also increases.

We have named and shall now describe some relationships that are surfacing today. Some of these are partnerships of the 90's that would have horrified our parents and grandparents. While most of these relationships do not end in marriage, some lucky ones do but the others offer temporary happiness to those involved. Sex may not have been the initial attraction but is often assumed to be an essential part. These living arrangements occur in all age groups but surprisingly, are becoming prevalent in the over sixty crowd that was raised with tighter moral standards.

The Unexpected Fling

This opportunity is usually not a planned event but happens spontaneously. It can involve two singles, two marrieds or one of each. With seniors traveling more than ever and not always with their spouse, the occasion often arises for an unexpected fling. Tour companies huddle their groups together and random singles seek each other out. What may be an innocent seat assignment, can be the beginning of an unexpected fling! Some tour companies now advertise partnerships for unattached males and females specifically for older travelers. Roommates are selected before the trip by mutual consent and have reportedly resulted in some marriages. On a recent trip we observed a married male, traveling without spouse in our tour group, fall into a relationship with a widow traveling in the same tour group. Although they were both very discrete, it was obvious within this small group of seniors that they had bonded. The group may not have individually approved of their relationship, but they were extremely tolerant. In conversations with the female of the couple, she made it clear that they had no future plans to see one another. He had a happy marriage to a wife who did not like to travel and they both accepted this as an unexpected pleasure with no further anticipations or regrets. Both had admitted to each other that under different circumstances, a future together was distinctly possible. It was an unexpected fling for both of them.

Professional Relationships

This relationship is one that develops through a non-social situation and often includes contact with a professional. The initial contact arises from a need, either real or emotional, and one party is usually seeking some kind of help from the other. While most professional contacts fulfill a distinct function, the potential for personal involvement is always there. Professional contacts do not frequently develop into personal relationships, but some do.

Counselors, including clergy, psychologists, psychiatrists and therapists of all kinds are in daily contact with distressed and disturbed people who are emotionally vulnerable. As counselors, they are involved with mental trauma, chemical addictions and a whole variety of aberrant behavior. A counselor has a dominant position in the contact with the individual seeking support. Through repeated counseling sessions, a bond may emerge between the two. They share confidences that may not be known to even their best friends. This deepens the bond and helps in the healing process. However, once the professional runs into the personal, a different relationship begins. If this involves a man and a woman, it can become sexual and if so, is usually detrimental to both. This can happen between clergy and their parishioners. Recently, a local minister became sexually involved with a grieving widow he was counseling. The affair lasted several months and was the talk of the congregation. He left the ministry but they no longer see each other.

The dominant role and the bond as discussed above, applies equally, if not more strongly to the doctor-patient relationship and to a lesser extent between lawyer and client.

A professional relationship is often established between a doctor and his patient during which personal habits, preferences and information are revealed previously known only to close family. The process of curing or alleviating symptoms possibly sets the doctor up as a "demi-god" to his patient. Because of this, the patient feels a strong bond with the doctor who has the power to cure. In this situation, it is easy to mistake admiration for attraction. Add a little chemistry, common interests and availability and the professional relationship can evolve into a personal relationship. Besides the patient, the door is open to establishing contacts with family members of seriously ill patients. Family members are extremely vulnerable at this time and often seek relief from doctors and other professional help around them. Care givers for the chronically disabled and terminally ill also fall into this category. The possibilities of entanglements are always there.

Seniors frequent a lawyer's office most often just after or just before a spouse's death. They are seeking legal advice at a time when they are very fragile and in need of support. Repeated visits are usually necessary. Death brings many legal problems. A trust must develop between lawyer and client that can grow and continue for long after. Again, it's another type of relationship and an opportunity for new companionship.

Business contacts, within or outside a particular firm, can be the nucleus for the initiation of social interaction. Business socializing has no boundaries like the corporate structure does. It provides a meeting ground for all levels and ages. The business relationship of the 1930's to 1940's was more or less restricted to the male boss and the female secretary. Not so now. Women now account for close to half of the work force and often work into their senior years. They are in all professions and at all levels of management. Despite this, their boss is often a man. A power struggle can often take place. If sex enters into the picture, it is instigated by senior men with younger women rather than senior women. Older women in senior positions are definitely capable of lusting after younger men but nothing like the frequency or intensity of older, male executives.

The term, May-December relationship, was common fifty years ago and refers to the mating of an older male and a much younger female. The "dirty old man" was obviously in the winter --December -- of his life and the young woman was in her springtime. This term has now been replaced with the expression "trophy wife" or "significant other".

Menage a Trois

Traditionally, this term refers to a household of three living in the same quarters. The term is from the French and was originally used to describe living arrangements of some artists on the left bank. Two women and one man was the usual combination. Although Frenchmen prefer to keep lovers separated, artists were often brought together by a shortage of money, rooming space and friendship. Sex was inevitable and tolerated by the artistic colony.

Today there are variations of this arrangement and they are often not living in the same house at the same time. Some are aware of another woman and some are not. Unlike the snowbird, who is looking for a new winter mate each year, today's menage has pre-selected two or more lovers who live permanently in different areas. Sometimes, they visit him but more often, he comes to them for an extended visit. After repeated visits, they become accepted as a couple in the social life of the community. After a time, he can have social contacts in several locations. If the menage is limited to only two women, they may be chosen mainly because of geography or climate. Money is always a factor and the extended visit can bring the money problems of daily living to the surface. Eventually, this type of arrangement becomes unacceptable for one of the three and it is usually one of the two women.

The following three relationships have similar characteristics but are different enough to be separated. Two of them are dominated by one of the partners, usually the male, who seeks a relationship but views it from the beginning as a temporary arrangement. However, this is not always made known to the partner. The "snowbird" looks for a new partner in his winter playground whereas the "geriatric stud" changes partners on his own turf. In the third relationship, both partners initially view their pairing as permanent.

"Snowbird" Relationships

By this term, we mean the temporary geographic relocation of individuals to a more pleasant climate as the seasons change. The term is more frequently applied to seniors in the northern states who flee to Florida and other warmer states to avoid the snow. The concept also applies to other areas of the country where retired singles temporarily move from harsh climates. Some spend half the year plus one day for tax reasons; some rent for three months and some only vacation there for a month or so. All are looking for quick companionship among other transient "snowbirds". There isn't time to develop long, social ties and the established community living there is already involved in their own activities. Choice of a location may depend upon the availability of senior sports but often is guided by a friend's advice. Seniors will seek out each other whenever possible but particularly when they are regarded as "snowbirds". Bridge and tennis players will seek partners and golfers will sign up for a foursome. Many become acquainted through welcoming get-togethers that are posted on condo bulletin boards and in elevators. "Early birds" at nearby restaurants are attended primarily by seniors. This dining group often develops into a nucleus for other social activities.

"Snowbird relationships" have a better chance of developing between traveling singles, widowed, married or divorced, who meet by chance and come from different locations in the North. This is the reason many of them travel south. Groups that travel together, generally stay together. Those within the group are inhibited from forming new relationships because they must return to their other life and are under constant observation by their close friends both at home and while vacationing. If the snowbird traveler is temporarily out of a relationship, then this does not apply and he/she is free to pick up a new partner in the South.

Singles can be involved in a new "snowbird relationship" every year. They can change location or partners or both. They are not seeking any type of permanent partnership, only companionship, sexual or otherwise, while they are enjoying a change of climate. Last year's companion may be old history this year. On the other hand, both may seek each other out the following year while retaining a significant other elsewhere. This arrangement can be delicate and difficult to continue over a number of years. For most people, sharing an intimate partner over time is deceitful, hurtful, and troublesome to seniors who grew up in a different generation. There is no way that jealousy does not eventually enter into this arrangement. Emotional stress, problems of money, living arrangements and family all surface in any continuing relationship of this kind.

Geriatric Stud/Forever Single

Persons in this group have a mindset against remarrying, no matter what, but intend to be involved in many relationships. There are undoubtedly a variety of reasons why men and some women, become geriatric studs. These reasons probably run the gamut from "second teenagehood," to unhappy first marriages and prolonged, difficult deaths of a first spouse or a messy divorce. Unhappy first marriages were often the result of an unplanned pregnancy and the social stigma attached if you did not get married many years ago. We did not socially accept single moms unless they were widowed. Whatever the reasons, there are many who fit into this group. There are probably geriatric studs in all groups with a "modern" relationship but at first glance, they may not be obvious. Presently, there are probably more males than females in this group but an increasing number of women also have no desire to marry or remarry at this age. The women today in all age groups are more independent. Those in our age group may be experiencing real independence for the first time, and after a year or two of single living, they are reluctant to give it up. They openly do not want marriage but they enjoy a good social life, would love a heterosexual relationship and do not want to be trapped socially into an exclusively women's group. Some social activities are couple oriented and with the shortage of males, unattached, independent women may be left out. Some women solve this problem by using escort services for social functions with no emotional involvement. Others may insure uninvolvement by using gay escorts, particularly as dancing partners. For the first time, women have learned to manage all aspects of their lives and no longer feel the need of a protective male or to be classified simply as "mother of" or "wife of". These women have found a new way to live, feel good about themselves and do not want to be encumbered with a steady partner, married or not. They finally have time to do everything they want to do without having to consult or compromise with anyone else. They have raised their families and are no longer responsible for their immediate care.

Jim and Sue have been dating for almost longer than either of them was married. Both are extremely sociable, attractive and like to do things together. Although Sue, from almost the beginning, intended that their relationship lead to marriage, Jim secretly never intended marriage to Sue or anyone. He enjoys being single again and as the years have passed, he became more strongly convinced that the single life is what he wanted. He enjoys being waited on, having a fun partner and an active sex life. They have separate residences. When the relationship appears to be getting too serious, he pulls away claiming family or other responsibilities. He has a beach house not far away that he can easily retreat to alone. This couple will never marry but may never end the relationship.

Some persons in this category may have many relationships in their late years and become more determined never to settle for just one. With the disproportionate number of females in this age group, males with such an inclination will have an easy time and probably find themselves in a paradise. The downside of this promiscuity is the increasing incidence of AIDS in this population of swingers. Some may also forget that age will finally take over and they will be alone in their failing years.

Revolving Relationship

This is a relationship that both parties, in the beginning, presume a commitment is in the future. It continues for an extended time, but when the breakup happens, it is permanent. Usually, there is an incompatibility that develops within the relationship that prevents any permanent arrangement. Most often, one of the partners needs and wants a lasting relationship. The other one really has no intention of committing to a marriage but has refused to admit this to his partner or even to himself. This is the difference between a revolving relationship and those we just discussed as the geriatric stud relationship. The geriatric stud hangs on as long as possible but when pressured toward permanent partnership, a breakup finally occurs. Friendship can still exist between the two after a breakup but may depend upon who broke it up and for what reason. For some reason it seems that women can usually maintain a friendship with an "ex" better than a man. Men consider a breakup that they did not initiate as a slight against their manhood. Feeling the need for a new partner, each party seeks another mate. This revolving relationship is very similar to the comfort relationship already discussed but sex is usually part of the revolving relationship but not necessarily in a comfort friendship. There is a real desire to be linked with someone and this is probably a reflection of previously long marriages or other relationships. Most people feel better with male/female companionship because there is always someone to do things with and somebody is there to care.

Seniors retire earlier than their parents did, often have pensions, continuing health insurance and when health permits, want a new life of activities they never had a chance to in earlier years. Freedom to live alone, travel, and develop new interests have become the way to spend our later years. Seniors are on the move more than ever. Lifestyles have so drastically changed that seniors are no longer limited to the role as a grandparent and the morals that they were raised with no longer exist. Our grandparents must be rolling in their graves!

Remarriage

The accepted adult relationship between female and male in all age groups is the married couple. Sex is considered an integral part of marriage. It is an accepted, anticipated activity and a symbol of love that binds the couple together. Non-married, sexual couples often have different values and either play by different rules, conveniently bend the rules or make rules as they go along. These are not bad people, they have just accepted the "new morality" and go with the flow.

Even though the decision to marry or not marry is a personal one, this decision is greatly influenced by the norms we grew up with as well as the reaction of friends and family around us. Our generation, which was raised in the days of the depression, is generally more conservative than our children. We were raised to follow rules and regulations set down by church, government and family. Those in this age group abide more by these rules than their sons and daughters. Though the moral fabric of society has drastically changed, it is much harder for us to live by the young people's (new) rules. We are more tolerant now of unmarried couples living together than we were even 15 years ago but we may not want to do it ourselves. Long-held religious and moral values certainly influence our decisions. Most religions disapprove of couples living together without the bonds of marriage.

Quoting the late Erma Bombeck, in a conversation with her daughter, Erma asked "why don't your friends get married...? The daughter replied: What difference does a piece of paper make? Erma's reply was, This isn't dating anymore. It's the major league of relationships. Maybe the difference between relationships and being married is the former is a spectator sport and the later is getting in the game and playing by all the rules."

Chapter 2

Why Are So Many Seniors Not Marrying?

Almost four hundred thousand seniors live outside the bans of matrimony.

Since so many seniors are living together in some type of relationship, we asked ourselves what are the reasons for this and are there common grounds explaining this new trend. Each couple has reasons of their own but most couples deciding against marriage base their decision on one or two overwhelming factors. These are **money** and **children.** Not far behind is another barrier----the **fear** of remarriage. On the other side, the recent **peer acceptance** of couples living together without marriage has been a big boost to this social change.

Money

If financial matters were the only factor involved, most couples in this age group would just live together. Fortunately, at this time society still expects better conduct from its mature citizens. However, the division of assets and dealing with future money can be a threat to any permanent, legal relationship. The money of a relationship includes home ownership, social security, pensions and survivor benefits as well as all other assets accumulated over a lifetime that each individual brings to the relationship. The legal aspects of dealing with these moneys mentioned above will be discussed in a later chapter.

For those over sixty, their home is often the largest asset they have. Because of this, most are extremely protective and possessive of it. It is not only a monetary asset but it is filled with a bundle of emotional memories. From the legal and tax side of the question, the answers have been made much simpler with the enactment of the Tax Relief Act of 1997. A couple contemplating marriage with two homes to sell will no longer have to deal with a one-time exclusion before being married. This new capital gains exclusion applies to all home owners regardless of age. The only qualification for the new exclusion benefit is that the house sold must have been the principle residence for at least two of the last five years subsequent to the date of the sale. It is not limited to a one-time sale as was previously the case. Before the new law, individuals were required to be 55 or older and were allowed a one-time capital gain exclusion of $125,000. The new tax law allows an exclusion up to $500,000 for couples filing jointly and up to $250,000 for single taxpayers.

The marriage penalty still flounders in Congress. It's discriminatory, unfair and greedy. It encourages couples not to get married. Social Security benefits are not taxed for individuals with incomes under $25,000 whereas social security benefits of married couples are taxed if combined income exceeds $32,000. Therefore, two senior singles living together can each receive $25,000 or a total of $50,000 in yearly income before their benefits are taxed. Social security benefits of a married couple are taxed after their combined incomes exceed $32,000. Marriage results in more of the benefits being taxed than if they remain single. In other words, a married couple is taxed on $18,000 more than two singles living together. This marriage penalty is currently being looked at by Congress, but so far they are dragging their feet, as usual.

Married people have the option of determining their tax burden as a single or a couple. The non-legal couple does not have this option. Singles generally pay taxes at a higher rate. If 70% of a married couple's income comes from one of the individuals, the couple's tax would be lower than if reported separately. If their incomes are fairly close, they would pay more tax than if they reported as singles.

Some pensions can be lost with remarriage. There are private companies that will exclude widowed and divorced persons from receiving pensions once they remarry or do not pay benefits after a certain age. It should also be noted for couples contemplating marriage, that retirees are not eligible to enroll new spouses into previously established benefit plans. Anyone contemplating marriage and retirement, should marry before retiring to assure survivor benefits for the new spouse. *Unmarried partners receive no survivor benefits no matter how long they have been living together.*

Here's an illustration of how money, or the lack of it, can cause dissension.

Martin and Mary started their relationship within the first year of their meeting, but after eight years it has not been legally finalized. They live and travel together, share daily expenses but each continues to own a separate residence. They are an attractive, gregarious couple with many friends and a busy social life. They have a good sexual relationship that is open and freely admitted by both. At various times, they have both considered marriage and have sought legal guidance but because of financial mindsets and disapproval of their children, they remain as a non-legal couple. The financial difficulties stem from the disproportionate assets of Martin as compared to Mary. He owns his own small, successful company that his children do not want shared. They cannot agree on a pre-nuptial agreement satisfactory to both and so remain comfortable as they are. As time goes on, the idea of marriage becomes less and less considered by both. It's no longer a frequent topic and they become defensive when it's brought up. The recent discovery of colon cancer in Martin and the family's instant takeover of his health care and financial assets came as a shock to Mary. Because of their non-legal relationship, she was not included in any of the major decisions. She was treated with disdain and when it came to discussions that effected his children, she was not consulted or included. It was almost as if his children feared that Martin and Mary's bond would become stronger and perhaps legally permanent as his health declined. They were afraid that he might want to use his assets to protect and care for her after he was gone. They never did marry but remained as strong a couple, as if they had, until he died.

Disapproval of Children

Probably the next biggest obstacles to remarriage at this age are children from previous marriages. Generally, children want their parents to be happy as long as it doesn't change their lives. They often view marriage at this age as a threat to their life style and a danger to their inheritance. It can impact on the time they share with their parent and now grandparent. Most have developed a life-long bond with their families. Grown children have often looked to their parent for financial support as well as baby sitting and helping with entertainment chores. They can be selfish and often think that no one is good enough to replace their lost parent. Children from either side of a relationship may wonder about mixing different religions or cultures. This is less of a problem at this age since sixty's plus persons are comfortable as they are and less likely to cross their established social lines. This also applies to interracial couples. Individuals, who have professionally worked together and are intellectually and economically at the same level, may not find this a problem. Years ago, interracial relationships were limited to the artistic crowd of writers, entertainers and painters. Now because they are not raising families, religion, culture and race are not the obstacles that they were in their youth. Families are more concerned about the social and educational levels of the potential spouse and how she or he would interact with the extended family. While any social or educational differences may not bother the senior couple, their children on both sides may disapprove of any social imbalance. They are in the social climbing phase of their lives and do not want a family addition who might embarrass them or not come up the their "inflated image" of themselves.

Children are also concerned about the health of the partner to be, especially if the new partner has major health problems or is significantly older or younger. An older partner is more likely to develop the problems of old age sooner. All health problems cost money and dig into potential inheritances. The increasing costs of health care can diminish the finances of anybody with illness.

There is an old Italian expression that inheritors should follow blood lines and not wedding bands. The issue of inheritance is always there whether it is talked about or not. Children are often too embarrassed to bring it up and parents do not like to talk about it. Couples living together with or without marriage make daily financial decisions that will affect an heir's legacy but nothing like the division of major assets. These can be easily managed by prenuptial agreements and wills that will be discussed later.

Rita and Joe met at a group function and were immediately attracted to each other. They dated several months before getting into a sexual relationship. The relationship didn't really bother their children as they had often engaged in similar activity but as the relationship continued and the possibility of marriage loomed, the atmosphere changed. Rita's children worried about loosing their inheritance. Rita inherited family wealth. Joe's children really did not like Rita's "airs" and thought that she was too old (10 years older) for their father. They reminded him that she was closer to a major health problem than he and their quality years might be few. Children are always interested in the health of the partner as no child wants to see his parent taking care of an invalid or care for someone with a long term health problem. However, the objections of Rita's children might have been motivated by their consuming desire to protect their inheritance.

Fear of Remarriage

Many older individuals who were widowed or divorced are fearful of trying marriage again. They prefer a non-legal relationship to marriage and feel safer as a single. Emotional strain, anger and financial stress of a failed marriage can create mental obstacles impossible to overcome. Fear of future health problems always exists in older people. The major chronic and fatal diseases peak in this age group. Avoiding them is almost a miracle.

Frequently, seniors want the companionship, with or without sex, the social activities of a mixed group but not another legal commitment. The depth of the fear often comes from the tragedy of the death of the spouse or the trauma of a divorce. As stated before, counselors have found that the sudden death of a spouse is accompanied by a longer recovery and readjustment period. A prolonged death allows the surviving mate to accept the inevitability of the end and therefore the grieving process starts during the illness. This same time frame can exist for divorced couples as well. Guilt does not usually follow the natural death of a spouse but often remains with divorced couples and contributes to their fear of a new commitment. The fear of again breaking up, whether it is caused by the death of a new spouse or another incompatible relationship, is stronger in a subsequent partnership than it was initially. The dread of again taking care of a spouse with a prolonged illness can often rekindle the fear and reluctance to assume once again the necessary responsibilities of caregiver. This is a natural reaction that is very understandable and is much more prevalent in new singles over sixty.

The introduction of a new relationship can disrupt established family patterns unless the new partner can almost fill the mold of the missing one. Differences between the new couple and their families can generate fear. These differences can be overlooked more easily in a "modern" relationship because no one is sure just how long the arrangement might last. Again, the fear of upsetting children and other relatives dampens the marriage prospects for a new, older couple. Social, religious and educational differences are easier to handle outside of marriage and can frequently be enough to prevent remarriage.

An example of the above can be found in our friends, Sally and Harry. They have each already been through a divorce in their early thirties and now in their 60's, they are divorcing again. Their children are grown and out of the house. Harry was playing around with a new marketing manager, who was recently divorced and in her early 40's. Fear that this could happen again, makes Sally believe that marriage is not for her but she feels she could go with a modern relationship. She might well consider a younger partner as her husband did.

Peer Acceptance -- *The Added Boost*

Jane and Mary met by accident while leaving Church one Sunday. Jane was a regular attendee at Church and had been widowed for over five years. Since they had not seen each other in over a year, pleasantries were exchanged and events were updated. Mary revealed that she had met an interesting man about six months before and that they were seeing quite abit of each other. Although she did not say they had a sexual relationship, it was obvious that they were intimately involved. Her parting comment concerning her "friend" was, "despite my upbringing, I looked around and saw that most of my single friends were involved in relationships like mine. This made it seem OK to me and soothed my guilty conscience."

The acceptance of sexual relationships among seniors now has the apparent approval of many of their peers. Both old and new friends seem to presume a sexual relationship exists between a dating couple. This apparent approval of peers is contrary to the standards of 30 years ago but makes it easier for a dating couple. Previously, this same couple would not think of a similar relationship without marriage. Does guilt interfere with the progression of a new relationship? This depends upon how long the parties have been single, how strong their moral commitment to marriage is and how family and friends approve of the relationship. Within the widespread practice of sexual relationships between senior men and women, there continues to exist the age-old male demand of sex as an accepted part of a relationship.

Does this mean that a senior relationship always has sex? Not always but generally, yes. It seems quite apparent to us that there is a female and a male side to this question. A male would eagerly answer yes to the sex question even if he has personal worries about his performance. Couples that are considered "going steady" are assumed to be in a sexual relationship whether they are or are not. The female learns that sex is often expected of her even if it is against her previous moral standards. The female may have been accustomed to getting along without sex and while she may long for intimacy, her body does not insist upon it and age has effected her desires as well. The woman, with her cluster of female and male friends, is protected from becoming involved in sexual relationships longer than the male. He more readily forages ahead in search of the single life he knew before and hopes to find again. With the abundance of single women in this age group, he has an easier time finding a mate. Curiously though, the male often fears rejection and for that reason depends upon a woman to draw him out into activities that might lead to a new relationship. It's been the traditional role of the wife of the 50's and 60's to be the social arranger for the family. Males are used to following their mate's lead and have become used to the role. The new morality can make it possible for couples to live together, buy property in two names, travel together in their own names and socialize freely as a couple with groups of legally married people. Society is making it easier for us to live like our kids.

Chapter 3

Wine and Cheese Get Better With Age----Do We??

Relationships are not the same at sixty plus because we have drastically changed and the rules have changed even faster. Any person thinking about dating in their 60's is quite different from they were in their twenties. We have a history behind us. Every situation, person and event, whether happy, sad, or tragic has touched us. These have all left marks and they continue to influence and direct our actions long after. We are different because those over sixty have probably already gone through at least one happy or not so happy relationship and/or marriage. Some may have gone through more with lasting scars of one or more divorces. The scars may be deeper than those of widowed persons because of the guilt associated with a divorce. The adjustment and survival time following divorce is emotionally and economically stressful and most women end up financially poorer than when they were married. If divorce came at an older age, the social adjustments are much more difficult. If abuse was the basis for the separation, then the abused individual would be extremely reluctant to be involved in another relationship. Divorce would not effect the abuser----he would just seek another mate.

Many have already faced the death of a spouse. In the case of sudden death, the impact on the survivor is different from that following a lingering illness. The surviving spouse now has the entire responsibility of the family that was previously shared. A long illness provides the spouse with time to accept the inevitable death. During this long, emotionally draining period, the survivor begins the grieving process before the actual death. Sudden death is catastrophic and a much more difficult situation for the survivor. The grieving time is usually much longer than after a prolonged illness. In either case, the over sixty person is probably alone after many decades of being in a partnership.

All these experiences are bound to have a dominate role in what a senior wants to do with the rest of his/her life and are perhaps the most important influence on future relationships. The "over 60" person already has had the opportunity to use whatever education he/she was given. Education affects our speech, dress, friends, work, outside activities and much more. Whether schooling was rural, urban, rich or poor, it usually controlled or influenced our social life and this factor continues well into retirement years. Educational background often determines social contacts throughout ones' life. The most significant character changes occur after high school and continue into our career years. However, retirement and more leisure time now seem to make continuing education a new goal for both men and women. They approach education with a different perspective now. Seniors study for pleasure rather than careers. Over the last 25 years opportunities for "over 60" education have exploded. Local educational facilities are supported by county and state universities, community colleges as well as private universities. Elderhostel has blended education with travel and this combination is hard to beat.

People at this age are influenced by their previous work experience but they are no longer actively involved in it. We are different because we have either already retired or are resting on a plateau that was attained before the age of 60. This plateau or career-high is often reached 10-15 years before retirement and its' influence on one's social environment is a major factor. It's hard to separate career levels and education as one often influences the other. Many do not socialize with fellow workers but if they do, it's usually within the same career status even if careers are in different fields. This applies to male and female relationships even after work years are over. There is a common bond that draws groups together even when persons are not actively involved in these areas anymore. Those in the sciences develop new friends who are scientifically oriented; artists and performers never lose these interests and those in sales find it easy to mingle from long experience in dealing with people. It's not only the career level that influences social activity but the type of work or profession and the hours that were worked that can make the "over 60's" person unique and different from what they were at 25.

Frequent job related travel can also have an influence. We are different because our diverse associations in different geographical areas have helped to broaden our interests and our personality. Someone from either coast that lives in the Midwest hopefully has acquired the best characteristics of both regions. Those at 60 may have already picked up characteristics from several different regions. We have become less provincial and more worldly. Travel and age have expanded our interests and often increased our sociability.

At this stage of retirement or pre-retirement, the time and energy devoted to a job should be redirected into new or ongoing hobbies or interests. Contrary to people in their twenties, most people over 60 have slowed down and may already be suffering from minor complaints and major diseases. Most cancer, heart disease and strokes occur around this age. Despite this, there are increasing large numbers of healthy, older individuals well over 60 with few or no complaints. These have recently been referred to as "robust seniors" and by the more cynical, as disgustingly healthy. Whichever group a senior falls into probably depends upon heredity as much as any other single factor.

As we age, interests change. What we were interested in at 25 is not necessarily what excites us at 60. We are now more spectators than the participant that we used to be. Our bodies now limit the type of physical sports that we are able to do. We have the time but not always the agility and endurance. However, there are many still actively engaged in swimming, tennis and biking. Because golf requires more time and less physical strain, it is an ideal recreation for this age group. Retirement communities are often planned around new golf courses. Newly built swimming pools frequently include Jacuzzi portions as well as areas designed for aerobic exercise classes. Ballroom dancing is even more popular in the over 60 group than with younger couples. At this age, you have the time to do the things you want rather than doing the things you have to do. Peer competition is at a minimum contrary to ones' earlier years.

We are different because, as we grow older, the family grows larger and often more complicated. Our children are now having children. These young adults may already have experienced divorce and re-marriage in their own lives. The "over 60" grandparent may now have grandchildren and step grandchildren and a potentially infinite number of in-laws. The social and legal complications of this are mind numbing. When the "60 plus" person was 25, these situations were rare rather than commonplace as they are now. Our parents did not have this challenge and have left many of us unprepared and ill equipped to handle these complications. These millennium families put many obstacles in the way of any new relationship. When a sixty plus person is left alone, the family becomes the most important support group to that person. While married or remarried, the spouse is the focus of the partner's attention. When one is alone, he or she looks to the extended family for entertainment and advice. The unmarried couple will revert to their respective families for the same support but not to the partner's family.

Those born in the 20's and 30's most often adopted and followed their parents beliefs longer than the youth of today. Many have never changed their religion or even considered changing it. Most individuals, now in their sixties, belonged to recognized religions of the day. Socializing was often church or synagogue centered and intermarriage between different religions was difficult for the couple and frowned upon by the families. Individuals in their 60's often have to deal with multi-religious situations that are often contrary to their own lifetime beliefs. We are molded by these factors at all ages but after 60, the effect of these moldings determines one's outlook toward his/her remaining years.

We can't change the results of our earlier years but we do have some control over our appearance in the years we have left. Ones' appearance is always changing but looking old is an impression of an individual's physical well being. Acting old is doing things in what's perceived as an "out of date "style. We are constantly making judgments about people as well as being judged ourselves. First impressions are often wrong but are still made. Here are some of the superficial factors that often characterize a person as being old. We all use these measurements every day even though we staunchly defend the way we present ourselves.

At a very early age, we start developing and wearing a style of clothing that makes us feel comfortable. It often projects what we think of ourselves. It is influenced more by our environment than our financial station. Mentally, if we feel good we probably look good. Through the years, most people become more conservative in their choice of clothing but still reflect their earlier likes and dislikes. Keeping up with fashion is not necessarily important, as we grow older, but being cognizant of changes and incorporating some into our life style is important. Very out-of-date clothes will tend to make us look older than we actually are. At any adult age, our appearance is always being compared to those that are younger. By our senior years, we should have learned what looks good on us and what does not. More than anything, we should learn to camouflage our deficiencies. No matter what style is worn, neatness and cleanliness must always be observed. Wearing torn or badly soiled clothing never gives a good impression. The casual (bummy) look of the younger generation may make them look "cool" but makes us look worn out.

Keeping up with flattering colors is worthwhile as your skin tones change and more wrinkles or expression lines appear. Expression lines have been deepening for more than half a century. After 60, they often signal our feelings more than we would like. We may be pre-occupied with unpleasant things, but everyone does not have to be aware of them. A smile is always better than a depressed look.

Although not usually classified as a makeup, both men and women are now using more of the sunless cremes in winter as well as in summer. Their use can give the appearance of health and fitness but overuse will have the same effect as any poor makeup. Still, this is a much healthier habit than sun bathing.

Both baldness and gray hair usually make a person look older. Neither situation is considered an advantage, especially to those in this age group. Women have been coloring their hair for centuries. Now we see men doing the same. Whatever makes an individual feel better about themselves should be their decision. Get advice about color and don't overdo any choice. Keep in mind that drastic changes require constant upkeep. This can be both expensive and bothersome. Remember your eyes are not as they used to be--and may not detect the old gray showing through. Hair thinning is a discouraging problem at this age for both sexes and choice of color should be considered with this in mind. Dark, thinning hair accentuates a light scalp.

Stooped people automatically look older. This may be caused by some physical problem that cannot be helped. However, many in this age group have developed poor posture over the years through habit more than anything else. We do not see ourselves moving as others do and our increased years have made rounded shoulders into a definite stoop. Instead of looking straight ahead, we tend to hang our heads low and watch the path even if we do not have to. Our body gestures and mannerisms express our mood. Standing tall is easier for the healthy young but has the advantage of making those that are older look more distinguished and confident.

Needless to say, either over or under weight tends to make anyone look older, less healthy and less vigorous. Most of the time, this is correctable, but when you are over 60, it takes longer and seems much harder.

Regardless of the age, appearance or health of a couple, it is important to keep in mind that every good relationship contains certain essential qualities. These qualities are all necessary but some are more important than others for individual couples. The list includes trustfulness, honesty, thoughtfulness, and dependability. Communication and compatibility are very important as well as love, joyfulness and happiness when the two partners are together.

Vitality means energy. It's equated with liveliness, vigor and animation. It's the driving force that keeps us young in spirit and mind. Vitality in this age group is very often diminished separately or by a combination of either age, depression, infirmity or to some debilitating disease. A vital senior citizen is almost always mentally and physically healthy or has overcome medical adversities.

Nobody is too old. We're used but not antique. We're wiser, stronger, more determined and aware that our lives are more than two-thirds over. Despite this, we have lots to give and share in our remaining years.

Chapter 4

Sex and Dating

Is it Still Possible? Still Enjoyable? Yes! Yes! Yes!

When a couple start dating at this age, their expectations are often quite varied. They reflect their past experiences and present new concerns such as "Am I too old to date?" "Am I still attractive?" "What will my children think?" "Do I really need this?" "What if he wants sex?" The dating process is different from when we were in our twenties, though the courtship period has many similarities. The thrill of finding a new partner at 60 plus seems even more exciting than it did at 25 but this excitement is tempered by an individual's previous experience. Dating choices should have qualities needed for a good mate rather than just a date. Look for a good friend rather than a good lover. We remain sexual beings regardless of our age. Above all, be yourself and decide beforehand, what changes you will accept. A single date can often tell a new couple that they really should not pursue the situation any further while another couple can be convinced that they should move ahead----as rapidly as possible. Age has made us wiser, more perceptive and definitely more selective in choosing friends or people we want to spend time with. Characteristics that have always been irritating, remain increasingly so. We know what works for us and time is always on our minds. If a couple finds they are compatible with some added "chemistry" they can progress into one of the relationships described in Chapter 1. Most couples develop a sexual relationship within six months of dating or earlier. The changing sexual morality of the 90's has been adopted by many of us in our 60's.

Many mature individuals, who have been sexually inactive for a period of time, may worry about resuming sexual activities. Healthy individuals at this age should have no physical limitations to an active sex life. However, psychologically, a barrier can exist for both parties. So much depends upon the individual's attitudes and what has taken place in their previous sex life. Were they happy and content with their relationship? Did they both enjoy sex? Did they express their feelings physically and verbally to one another? All this will bear upon their response to a new partner. Communication between the two parties can eliminate some of the worry and stress of this subject but only if both parties can talk freely about their feelings. Many cultures find it easier to express themselves. They communicate with gestures, facial motions and physical touching. Latin and southern European countries openly embrace and communicate by non-sexual touching. It's easier for them to share their sexual feelings than it is for most North Americans and Northern Europeans. We grew up with the idea that sex was private, secret and for reproduction, not pleasure. As a result, many feel this same way, even in a doctor's office. This is often because of family and religious upbringing and is more likely in the 60 plus age group than in their offspring. Sharing sexual experiences in conversation is common place among the young. Pointed questions are asked and answers freely given. Those in our generation, particularly the females, shy away from sharing the details of sexual encounters. Sexual talk among seniors rarely takes place and then only jokingly. Sexuality is much more than a physical act. One cannot choose not to have sexuality--it is a part of the fabric of one's life. We can choose not to have sex but we will always be sexual beings.

Once a couple has entered into a sexual relationship, there are definite advantages to sex after sixty. Couples no longer have to worry about unwanted pregnancies. Travel and leisure time create a more romantic atmosphere. Generally this group has more leisure time and more money to pamper themselves. The absence of children provides more time alone as a couple. Love making does not have to be at nighttime when all the children are in bed. A new couple at this age brings a variety of techniques and experiences to their love making. They must adapt to each other and agree on not only what gives them pleasure but also shying away from aspects of sex that never made them happy.

A couple we know in our age group, has shared with us the fact that they have more morning and oral sex than each had in previous marriages. This has proved pleasurable to both even though it is a change from previous habits. Another couple admits to having infrequent sex but shares loving and emotion through hugging, kissing and touching.

If you have never been one to venture into adventurous sexual practices, this is probably not the time to start. However, don't close the door completely upon being more experimental both in and out of the bedroom. Sex among seniors is less gymnastic and experimental but generally more comfortable. We lean toward the habitual and familiar ways. Our relationships are more caring than lustful and definitely less performance oriented.

In the 90's, we have been exposed to what we did not grow up with ---- sex education for the adult. We are being exposed to people like Dr. Ruth and been educated sexually about better sex for yourself and your partner. Book stores have whole sections that contain "how to" books on any

37

aspect of sex for all ages. Some of the books are partially or completely devoted to geriatric sex. Many of the movies show sex as being an expected part of life. Some current movies rated PG13 could make seniors blush. Magazines and periodicals always have at least one or more articles related to our bodies, intertwined with a sexual angle. "Kinky" sex, which was usually not a part of our upbringing, rears its' ugly head even in the senior population.

A survey conducted by the AARP, and published recently in their September - October 1999 issue of Modern Maturity, shatters some of the myths about seniors and sex. Roughly two thirds of those surveyed were very satisfied with their sex life. Although their sample included groups under the age of 60, we will limit our comments to those over 60. The survey points out that as seniors' age, the number of individuals with sexual partners decreases rapidly, especially for females. Just under 50 per cent of men and women with partners have sex at least once a week and the majority are satisfied with their physical relationship. Better health heads the list for improving the sex life of men over sixty. When men have better health, the sex is better for both. The above facts show that while frequency drops with age, the satisfaction remains.

A 1996 survey by Parade magazine, studying sex after age sixty-five found substantially the same percentage of participants, frequency and satisfaction as the AARP survey. A 1998 survey commissioned by the National Council on the Aging came to similar conclusions. They further noted that hugging, kissing and intimacies are still important and older men and women seem to do better with looser sexual schedules. Sex in the afternoon, before dinner or in the morning often works better.

What do older men and women do in bed? The majority enjoy sexual intercourse more than foreplay. On the other hand, most enjoy hugging and more than half take pleasure in kissing and touching their lover's body. The Parade survey reported that seniors had an orgasm on an average of 7 out of 10 times and reached climax sooner than their younger counterparts. This is directly opposite to the assumption that older means slower. Many more women than men do not reach orgasm. Almost a third of the seniors use some item or device to enhance their sexual enjoyment. Of these, 81% use a lubricant during sex, especially women.

The downside of sex at this age is the number of conditions that can interfere or diminish sexual activity. The majority of these are more prevalent in males and impotency, which increases with age, heads the list. **Impotency** or erectile dysfunction (ED), is probably the biggest drawback to starting a new intimate relationship. Men who have not been sexually active for several years may fear that they can no longer function in bed. It is estimated that over half the male population over the age of 60 have some moderate to severe degree of impotency. Many in this population have physical reasons for being impotent but a large portion of men is more psychologically impotent than physically impotent. There are a number of causes of impotency that are difficult to treat, particularly in individuals with diabetes and hypertension. These diseases affect the blood circulation to the penis and therefore impede erection. Drugs, especially some used to treat hypertension, are another major cause of impotency. There are newer drugs that do not cause impotency but the drug must first be able to control the hypertension without regard to the side effect of impotency. The doctor's primary concern is to control the high blood pressure that is potentially life threatening. Smoking and alcohol have the same effect but can be more easily reversed with moderation or abstinence. Controlling smoking and drinking helps promote a healthy relationship that at a later date could become intimate. Impotency can be treated with implant surgery, vacuum erection systems, and drugs that are self injected into the penis before intercourse. Impotency is generally treated by a urologist but some cases can be treated by a psychotherapist. Clinics, dealing with impotency, are widely advertised on radio and in the lay press. Recently, Viagra has been excessively marketed to the population, with Bob Dole as the spokesperson for erectile dysfunction, and every senior is able to recite two or more jokes about it.

Some drugs taken by both sexes can diminish sexual desire. Two thirds of the respondents in a recent poll reported taking some kind of medication. Half of the men and one fifth of the women on medication said that the drugs had affected their sex life. Alcohol consumption, which frequently diminishes with age, can be a major problem, especially for men. A large consumption of alcohol can increase sex desire and decrease sexual performance of the male by inhibiting erection. Alcohol dilates the blood vessels of the penis, inhibiting an erection or making it difficult to sustain one.

Older couples may handle the problems of impotency in different ways. Here are some examples that we have encountered.

Both unmarried partners had an immediate affinity for each other but were resisting any sexual activity. She had some moral considerations concerning sex and he believed himself to be impotent but until now had no reason to change it or challenge it. He had been a heavy drinker earlier in life and this may have had some bearing on his physical ability. He had seriously considered an implant to fulfill his masculine desires but it was not until he was encouraged by his new partner, that he decided upon the operation. She had tried to help him get an erection with oral and manual stimulation but was not successful. They openly discussed the situation and he sought medical advice. After some careful thought by both, they made the decision together that he would have an implant to correct his impotency. The operation was successful and they have had a good sexual life and a continued partnership for many years now.

Here's another example of adjustment to impotency.

A male spouse of a couple married over 40 years developed impotency after several serious illnesses. His inability to participate in intercourse became an emotional issue between them as he did not think it was fair to his wife to deprive her of her sexual life. Their love was strong and she did not feel the urgency that he did. Although she did not encourage him or feel it was necessary to their relationship, she knew it was important to him. She supported his decision to get a vacuum condom.

Any type of cancer in either partner can be destructive to sexual activity. The reason is probably a combination of physical and psychological factors. A prime example of psychological trauma follows major breast surgery in a female. The psychological effect of surgery can exist long after the physical healing has taken place. This trauma can follow a hysterectomy even though a woman's sex life should not be affected by this procedure. Cancer of the prostate is being diagnosed and aggressively treated much more frequently than ten years ago. Many of the treatments potentially lead to temporary or permanent impotency. This does not mean that every male treated will be unable to have sex again. Generally, surgery on any of the primary or secondary sex organs of either male or female is bound to have some effect on a couple's sex life at any age.

Besides cancer and its treatments, heart disease can diminish the desire and performance of either the male or the female. Bypass surgery in itself should not prevent a normal sex life. Following surgery, the male may feel apprehensive about resuming sex and although this feeling is common, there is no medical reason for it. However, some men can become psychologically impotent.

Because seniors do not have to worry about birth control, a lot of older men and women with new sex partners do not think about safe sex or use condoms. Yet, 10% of AIDS cases involve people over the age of 50. The most common change made by women in light of AIDS is to abstain from sex while men decrease the number of sex partners.

Use of hormones for women has been a much debated issue and can affect the sexual drive of females. Although most women benefit from taking hormone replacement therapy to prevent health problems that confront women in the post menopausal years, it is not for everyone. This is a decision for each woman to make in conjunction with her gynecologist. A woman's sexuality does not have to be affected by menopause. If a woman had regular sexual relations before menopause, she will probably remain active throughout and after menopause. Difficulties with sex due to loss of estrogen may occur but can be treated with estrogen creams or lubricating jellies. Sexual relations often become more desirable at this stage of life. A woman and her partner have more time for each other and are also more experienced sexually and know how to please each other.

The most common reasons for the decline in sexual satisfaction in later life are cited as medical problems, old age, impotence and the lack of a partner. *The key factors for an improved sex life are a remarriage or a new partner, having a good or understanding partner and feeling more relaxed with less pressure.* While there are possibly more men than women that want multiple partners at his age, physical conditions may force them to settle for one woman at a time. The problems among women are low sex drive, difficulty achieving orgasm and self-consciousness during sex.

The primary reason for the difference of sexual activity between men and women is that many more women than men find themselves without partners after the age of 65. There are three females for every male in this age group and in some areas the ratio is much greater. In order to deal with this, women may have to become more cautiously aggressive and might even consider the possibility of sharing a man if they can find one robust enough. Women may want to share a partner for different activities without full sexual involvement. There are both males and females that don't want to get sexually involved and prefer limiting sexual contacts to kissing, hugging, and petting. This might be easier for both partners as robust men are hard to find at this age.

Masturbation is probably the most frequent compensation for lack of intercourse. More males than females need this kind of compensation at this age. Some individuals can be content with hugging, caressing or mild petting. Oral sex is an acceptable alternative to intercourse particularly if both parties enjoy it. Males are capable of having an orgasm even when they are partially or not at all erected. This gives them satisfaction and calls for a hands-on approach or oral sex. Sex enhancers such as body lotions, perfumes and massage oils help add to the mood and increase the pleasure of sex. Sex videos are readily available for rent or purchase from almost any video store. Reading pornographic literature has been used for years as a compensation for intercourse as well as stimulation.

For the hardy, there are available a variety of "sex toys" that can be used on or by females.

Whatever means a person chooses, couples in a relationship should endeavor to make their partner's pleasure and satisfaction their primary goal.

Chapter 5

Problems Facing New Couples

There are a number of problems, personal or otherwise, facing new couples that are different from those encountered by couples who have been together for many years. These problems are their inclusion or exclusion in social circles, housing decisions, attitudes of spending, family acceptance, deteriorating health and adapting to each other at this age.

Although peer acceptance of the non-married is an advantage for many couples, it does not always happen. Many married groups still do not include the unmarried. This forces unmarried couples to socialize with singles or other unmarried couples. There are many geographic and cultural areas that exclude these couples but then there are others, such as California and Florida, where nobody cares one way or the other. Every month the barriers between non-married couples living together and married couples are disappearing. This is copying the pattern that so many young people have already put into practice. The seniors, however, do not have to worry about having children as the young do, but have their own set of worrisome problems.

Housing Decisions

We will discuss the various living arrangements that are available to new couples. This includes those intending to get married, those that are not sure and those that are sure they don't want to marry. Where to live and what to do with two or more residencies have always been a problem for new, mature couples. The decision making process involving a home with its years of memories is often harder emotionally than the financial side. Each partner has a house full of family history and if it's a home that has raised a family, decisions are even more difficult.

One of the first questions a "new couple" has to face is whether they want to be together all the time. If being together all the time is their choice, then they must first decide where they are going to live. Most individuals at this age have mortgage free dwellings or are renting apartments at reasonable rates. A couple must decide whether to keep both residences or occupy just one. The tax situation concerning home ownership has already been addressed. Seniors remain very aware of what is theirs' and what they may leave to their respective heirs. Home buying decisions are often guided by the couple's children who are worried about their inheritance. This problem can be handled easily through legal, prenuptial agreements if marriage is contemplated. Alternately, they can sell or rent one, live in the other or sell both and buy a third. Unmarried couples might choose to retain their individual homes as a hedge against a breakup.

Even though living together without marriage is more acceptable than twenty-five years ago, the mature citizen may not feel comfortable with this arrangement and be embarrassed in front of his or her children. Children may think living together is all right for themselves but be embarrassed for a parent. Old married friends may socially exclude both parties. An alternate solution is to get married which can be terrifying to many at this age. This is one of the reasons why many seniors establish relationships without marriage. They live mainly in one location but each retains his own residence. One aspect of this arrangement can be the obvious security each has if the relationship fails. A couple that made a fast, bad, decision to live together can retreat easily when a breakup occurs. By going back and forth between two homes, both parties are able to keep up with social contacts and neighbors surrounding their own home. They can seek selective solitude from their partner on their own property and most importantly, each property is preserved for future family inheritance as well as all the furniture and keepsakes. Finally, the financial arrangements for the couple are simpler as it really comes down to shared daily expenses. All major and minor house maintenance expenses are paid by each home owner.

A variation of this arrangement, is unmarried people who definitely don't want to get married. These unmarried couples have monogamous, sexual relationships but spend as much time in their own home with friends and family as they do with their partner. Although they spend time at each other's homes, they are not always together and are not considered a couple with any prospect of marriage. These are people who definitely don't want to get married and just can't take too much togetherness with their partner. They do not want to be pressured into something that they really don't want. If they really wished to be together most of the time, they would choose one place. The couple, living together in two houses, have established a relationship but, for their own reasons, do not wish to solidify it or to take it any further than their social, sexual encounter. They feel comfortable holding onto their own houses even when they are not always occupied. They may have sold their larger, family residences in exchange for something smaller but they continue to own separate dwellings.

Your Place or Mine? Which One? Once the decision has been made to live at one residence only, one party must give up their dwelling. It's important to remember that a dwelling was a *home* to one family which makes the decision harder and always emotional. The home to be let go must be either sold or rented. If sold there are no current tax problems to be contemplated. If rented or sold, moneys could be used to support the chosen home. If both parties had lived in rental apartments, the choices are simpler.

Often a couple will find one location easier than another to establish themselves as a new couple. As one's residence was often dictated by work, now family and close friends are the primary factors. The proximity of immediate family of either partner is very important. The ability to see children and grandchildren is probably one of the biggest determinants of where a couple will live. Other factors will come into play in deciding which residence the couple will use. An unmarried couple may find it difficult to be socially accepted in a neighborhood where one previously lived with a former spouse. The size and type of residence that each has are also determining factors for both the married and the unmarried couple. Whether one lives in a single family neighborhood (particularly one where one party has lived for years with another partner) versus an apartment or condominium with few compatible neighbors, makes a difference. The size of each home as well as the daily upkeep required by each are things that need to be considered. If one partner has long standing membership in a group such as Church, Country Club, Civic or Fraternal or Professional organization, then strong consideration should be given to building on these existing ties, as long as the group accepts them as a new couple. Despite the variety of factors, women seem to have stronger emotional attachments to their homes than the men. Years of nesting with child rearing, decorating and cooking have left them with strong bonds for their homes and possessions. Men love their homes but consider them more a place to live and a financial asset.

Both parties should realize that in order to make the chosen house a home, the new home must have cherished items from both houses. Since possibly more than half of the contents of each household must be disposed of, this process requires tact and understanding of each other's feelings. Often the couple will find that the children do not want the discards and are more interested in the possessions they have selected to keep. Attics and basements are often filled with memorabilia of the adults as well as their children. The children may have already taken what they wanted from their treasure of souvenirs and are not interested in clearing out the rest of their junk. Many of the charity organizations do not want them either. Discretion should be used in selecting family photos that include previous partners, living or dead. Any kind of a "shrine" to a previous spouse should be definitely discouraged but pictures and small keep-sakes should be supported.

For unmarried couples, financial arrangements must be discussed and resolved before one residence becomes the home of the couple. If the home ownership remains in one partner's name, payment of expenses should be shared but not necessarily equally. Since only one house is now lived-in by the couple, a lodging /rental contribution should be made to the owner. Monthly household expenses should be shared as well as minor maintenance. This is usually not a problem since they have already been sharing such costs. However, the problem of who pays for any major household structural upkeep and appliance repair and replacement, should be described in writing beforehand. Included in this document should also be remodeling and redecorating expenses, payment of property taxes and home owner's insurance. In the case of newly married couples, a premarital agreement, which is discussed later, should cover all the financial arrangements regarding housing.

Making a Fresh Start--Selling Both Homes This is a choice that serious, trusting partners may choose. This option is not uncommon for a couple planning to get married. It is seen more frequently in younger couples who have a longer lifetime to make changes, than those in our age group. If the couple decides to buy only one home, it is usually bought in joint title.

The advantages of starting fresh are many. The couple has discovered a new life together and can now share their tastes and fantasies in designing or selecting the home of their dreams. He may have always longed for a bigger workshop and a library/den for all his books. She may have dreamed about a bigger kitchen and a larger garden. Both may have thought about bigger bathrooms and closets galore. The thrill of looking and planning their new home can be exciting for both of them. Buying a new home eliminates the struggle in trying to decide which house to live in and leaves behind old memories of previous loves. New furnishings can be purchased in addition to each partner bringing selective, non-threatening possessions to decorate their new home.

Buying one new home may be enough for most couples, but there are some that may choose a second home as well. As they have each sold their primary residences, they may each want to buy something new and use one as a vacation or a get-away house. Both homes can be jointly titled or each partner may title one in his or her name. As we grow older, warmer climates become more desirable. The aging population of the southern states was the younger population of the Northeast fifty years ago. "Condo canyons" obliterate most scenic views and any remaining desirable land has been replaced by a golf course. It seems that in order to receive social security, you must have a golf bag and clubs. There are frequent "snow birds" who like to rent for the winter but they are considered in a separate category by the permanent residents. It is often difficult to be socially assimilated into an established, old community as a part-time resident. Those buying a home, even as a vacation home, might find it easier to socialize in a newly developed community, whether retirement or not. This allows them to be in areas where the majority of people are newcomers.

Should We Move to a Retirement Community? Moving to a retirement community is smarter for the unmarried couple than moving into an established community. Most residents relocated there after they turned 60 and retired. This is very different from moving to an established community which has little turnover and different concerns from those of the senior citizen. A retirement community presents a more comfortable life style at a time when one is most needed. They have a variety of living arrangements----single family, townhouse and high-rise condo models. The communities are self-contained with shuttles to nearby shopping and professional facilities. They provide total security along with accommodations for increasing disabilities of the aging residents, often being affiliated with hospitals and nursing homes as well as assisted living. Because units in these villages are maintained by the association, there is no need for lawn mowing, painting or plumbing repairs. Those living there have more leisure time to participate in a variety of social activities. Residents welcome newcomers and they are often looking for a new golf, tennis or bridge partner. Social directors plan parties, dances, game nights and sporting events. A retirement community is defined by age and even though married couples are part of the community, singles and unmarried couples abound. New residents sense the existence of other unmarried couples who are pleasant and helpful. These couples are paired in various types of relationships and offer instant camaraderie to a new couple. The people that move to retirement communities are generally a very active, social bunch. They are "do-ers" and anything but sedentary. The sedentary don't make moves at this time of their lives unless it's to assisted living housing.

Renting remains another option. Both homes may be rented and the proceeds used to rent or buy a third home for the new couple. This preserves the ownership of both houses and eliminates arguments about inheritance. It's an easy, simple solution to prevent costly mistakes. More importantly, it does not have to be permanent. They can try out different locations and climates before buying. Social compatibility can be judged before any real money is spent. Married couples, however, may want something more permanent. The opportunity to share a vacation home with children and grandchildren may be very appealing and more easily arranged with buying rather than renting.

The popularity of *shared housing* with unrelated persons has increased in recent years. Couples in a relationship of the same intensity, whether married or not, might contemplate shared housing for a variety of reasons. Compatible life styles, interests and hobbies as well as the obvious economic factors could lead couples into this arrangement. The sociability and companionship between the couples are definite advantages of this sharing. In addition to couples, we have seen more of this among senior retired, compatible women who as singles are as much interested in companionship as economy.

The disadvantages of such shared housing are obvious. The difficulties of running a household composed of four to eight persons who are already set in their different ways is an organizational nightmare. If one of the couples is a natural leader, this may solve the problem unless the others are not followers. Regardless of the best organized plans, each couple wants to do their own thing and schedules are often ignored as individuals this age don't want to be told what to do.

Another type of shared housing that causes potentially fewer problems is the joint ownership of a vacation residency. For example, four couples (married or not) purchase a vacation condo and share purchase and maintenance costs equally. All names are listed on the deed. Occupancy time is drawn by lottery and then rotated for prime months. Day-to-day costs are carried by the occupying couple and yearly golf and sports memberships are paid by the group. It is another option to be considered.

Attitudes of Spending

As we said, everybody is different at 60----all the past experiences that have brought us to this age are unique to each person. We have been molded by at least fifty years of living. Every situation, person and event whether happy, sad, or tragic has touched us. These have all left marks and they continue to influence and direct our actions. Money has always been one of the strongest factors directing us and may play a big part in how easily we engage in a new relationship in our older years.

Attitudes of spending are more important than the amounts we spend. How do we feel about the use of money? Do we feel that money should only be spent for practical things? Can we feel good about spending money on frivolous things occasionally? Do we still keep a rigid budget? Many couples find that their spending patterns are diametrically opposite. Almost anyone can get at least one credit card but people use them differently. Some feel that their credit line is the amount that they are allowed to spend with a lifetime to pay it back. These people pay the minimum amount monthly and never really intend to pay off their debt in full. This is more characteristic of the younger generation, many of whom have good incomes but their desires exceed their cash flow. Other people put every thing on a credit card and are systematic about paying it off each month. There are others who use credit only for emergencies. They deal in cash as a means of budgeting the amount of money they wish to spend at a particular time. Partners with opposite spending habits can have trouble in their new relationship.

Seniors now have more money to spend on themselves. Most have already fulfilled their major financial obligations-- education, house and car. Contrary to their parents, they are more savvy investors. Their knowledge and use of stocks, bonds and other investments often is greater than their parents. They have become their own investment advisors via the internet. Online investing and day trading are becoming a daytime recreation for some retirees. Seniors have more disposable income than at any other time of our lives. Though still conservative in their spending, many have become more self indulgent. While becoming more extravagant with ourselves, we are looking more to the care of our future and readily investing in long term health care insurance. This guarantees that we are taken care of and protects our assets. It keeps us independent from often complicated, extended families. *The assets of singles living together are treated separately and only the sick partner's moneys must be used for this care.* Long term care insurance, when added to retirement income, is usually sufficient to cover long term needs either at home or in a nursing home and preserve their assets for heirs. The majority of women and possibly a third of all the men who are now age 65 will spend their last years in a nursing home. The average cost of these facilities is at least $40,000 a year. Therefore, when looking for a long term care insurance policy, one should keep in mind that the policy should cover nursing homes as well as all levels of care, including assisted living and in-home care. Special attention should be paid to the duration of the contract that can extend from two years to a lifetime. Scrutiny should be given to the daily benefit amount, inflation protection and the age of the person applying. Anyone over 72, probably should not consider the need for an inflation clause. If one is fortunate enough to set aside roughly $160,000 at compound interest above what he wants to leave to heirs, just to pay for his care, he does not really need this kind of insurance.

Another method available to protect assets is the transfer of property to family members. This must be done three years before they apply for Medicaid nursing home benefits. Most seniors are hesitant to transfer ownership of their assets, accumulated over a life time, to a family member despite their close relationship. This might seem strange, but transferring assets is a form of losing ones' independence. *Independence is the last thing that seniors want to lose.* Even though many choose not to protect their assets this way, they are definitely thinking of their final years and "squirreling away" in their own sometimes secret ways.

Although financial arrangements of housing have already been discussed, everyday expenses are another concern for the unmarried couple living together. Since each has varied sources of monthly income, a plan must be worked with flexibility to cover daily expenses and monthly bills. A specified pool of money must come from both parties and is best handled by one or the other. If both individuals are "alpha" types, the task should be rotated. Entertainment expenses should be covered with pooled money. If feasible, an emergency fund should also be established and not raided.

The funding of trips is often a major source of friction for new couples. This can apply to all trips whether they are for pleasure, family visits or family emergencies. Often one or the other is reluctant to commit money for a trip that they are only lukewarm about but do so to appease the other party. Trips to the family of one are often in this category. The non-family member often chooses not to go or not to contribute. This can turn into an awkward situation for a loving couple and their children. Most children do not want to explain why grandma and her friend do not visit together.

Our *"gift giving"* patterns, which were set up many years ago, can create resentment when the pattern is broken or altered. Gift givers have many different personalities. There are those that are generous, those that are thrifty and others that feel the spirit of the event is more important than the actual gift itself. Each new couple must decide which category they fall into and whether a compromise is needed. They must decide who is going to receive gifts, are they going to be joint gifts and more importantly, who is going to pay for them. The larger the families, the bigger the problem, especially if one partner has many more children and grandchildren than the other. The female partner of an unmarried couple that we know, wrapped 73 gifts for his side of the family last year. Her only comment was, "Never again----next year it's going to change."

Using previously acquired assets can be a problem for any new couple. Any major expenses should be shared by both if their assets are similar. If dissimilar, then a compromise should be reached. Spending family assets applies only to the more permanent non-married couple but not to a fleeting relationship. In either case, the children of both sides should be left out of the discussions. Parents should still be able to spend their own money as they desire.

Family Problems

We love our families .....But! *The newly extended family of a relationship probably causes as many problems as money.* From the time that the new couple starts dating, the family becomes a central part of the relationship. By the family, we mean all the close relatives from both sides, their families and the significant others who may be temporarily involved. The numbers and the variety of personalities can be intriguing at the beginning but may become increasingly complex. Dealing with them all can be daunting since the family now is often twice as big as each partner had previously. We now have more time but less energy than when we were younger, yet we have more commitments to more "family."

Each family has a lifetime of traditions that become more prominent and emotional around religious holidays, birthdays, anniversaries or other family events made special over time. Where does the new couple go at Christmas? How about the traditional family vacation at the shore? Is the new couple expected at all the grandchildren's birthday parties? Should we visit our children equally regardless of their distance from us? All these questions have to be resolved without stirring up emotional outbursts and rivalry between the families. The essential ingredient in solving these dilemmas is a large amount of love and a larger amount of compromise. The new couple must now divide themselves between the combined total number of children. It was often hard to divide yourself among your own family but now it's twice as hard. The larger the family, the harder it is. All this scheduling must be done at the same time that the new couple is trying to establish their own traditions. These new routines and traditions become the foundation of the new couple's relationship and whatever patterns evolve regarding these special occasions will be hard to change in the future. In addition to holiday time, other time must also be shared with the extended family. The proximity of children and grandchildren often dictates the quantity of visits. Children and grandchildren at a distance also desire visits with their respective parents and any new partner. For families at a distance, with young children, school hours and working moms and dads, grandparents with new partners will probably have to travel more. Most grandparents want to see their grandchildren grow up and be able to pass on to them some insights about their heritage. They want to be able to help guide their growing up without interfering. Grandparents are permitted to spoil grandchildren. The parents have the duty to discipline them. As long as both do their own thing well, they should not clash and the grandchildren will have the best of both worlds. Grandparents are usually willing to give generously of their time and money.

Unmarried couples living separately face a different set of problems. They usually celebrate holidays and special events with their respective families. This is probably due to the fact that their lack of a legal commitment to each other reflects where their primary loyalties lie. The unmarried couple still allow their children to make these decisions for them. The married couple make the decisions themselves and the children no longer expect them to visit separately on holidays that are important to all concerned.

Those living together in one residence may face the same dilemma that the married couples do but with the added problem of children's disapproval of their living arrangements. This can further complicate family get-togethers. Many parents can acknowledge to young children that a grandparent has a special friend but don't really want to explain their intimate living arrangements without marriage. For this reason, unmarried couples may be requested to sleep separately while visiting. We always try to shield our young people during their most vulnerable years by setting standards and giving good examples that are sometimes loftier than we are practicing. Non-conventional living arrangements can be hard to explain to young children. For example, an unmarried couple we know still has emotionally upsetting times over the holiday season after several years of living together. Last year, she spent Christmas Eve with his family and then traveled to Oregon Christmas morning, alone, to be with her family. Neither partner wants this pattern to be repeated next year but are without a solution so far. They may never solve all the problems of holiday visits as easily as married couples can, but they will get through each hurdle as it comes along. As they want to establish their own routine, they are seriously considering a trip together away from both families during the holiday time. An unmarried couple can easily solve sticky family problems by traveling frequently and having a "planned" trip that interferes with potentially unpleasant family get-togethers.

Besides the gift giving factors of who gets, who pays and from whom, we found other interesting customs that may surface. Some people believe that gifts received for an occasion should be opened on the day of the event with loved ones around. Others feel that gifts and cards can be opened as soon as they arrive without ceremony. Christmas

Eve and Christmas Day offer different examples of gift opening traditions. Some families continue old world traditions involving Christmas Eve as the primary festivity and gift giving time. Other families with young children more often follow the Santa Claus tradition and hold their gifts and family gathering 'till Christmas day. All faiths have their own gift giving traditions that must be respected and observed.

There is no best way in gift giving. New patterns with compromise can be assimilated and new traditions established. This should be every new couple's goal.

There are other equally stressful problems involving both family and money. An unmarried partner may have an adult child who is dependent on financial aid for housing, academic degrees or anything else. The other partner may heartily disagree with this arrangement and not want it to continue if it compromises the activities of the new relationship. While it might be easier to cut off or limit support of an adult child, most would find it much more difficult to drop assistance for an aging parent. If either the adult child or the aging parent lives with one of the partners, the mood of the unmarried couple can easily be influenced. In any case the situation should be a "warning sign" and all caution taken beforehand. If the situation is fully understood and agreeable to both partners and family, conflicts can be minimal.

Deteriorating Health

Everybody's health at this age is deteriorating and relatively few people die in their sleep. Married couples accept this as part of growing older but partners in new relationships may not be as accepting and not want to be tied down. Although the legal responsibilities rest with the ill partner and immediate family, emotional caring and understanding should be shared by all. Daily care is frequently left to the partner, married or not. This is sometimes overlooked and ignored by the family, particularly if they have not accepted the relationship.

Established activities and the social life of the unmarried couple may be drastically changed by the illness of one of the partners. If one of the couple is confined to a hospital or rehabilitation center for an extended time, all social activities will come to a halt. However, if an individual has to move into assisted living or a nursing home, the unmarried partner is free to seek another relationship. Married couples may have more family support than unmarried couples in facing this situation. Both partners in a non-married relationship should be aware that medical and legal authority rests with the ill partner and his family.

Even without any major health problem, driving can be limited or completely restricted. This can cause problems for any couple because the ability to drive is extremely important and is one of the last manifestations of senior independence. Many mature individuals visibly deteriorate after losing their driver's license. At this time, a good relationship with a backup driver comes in handy.

Adapting

New couples, married or unmarried, have a "honeymoon" period at the beginning of their relationship. For those who do not get married, we will call it "the honey" without the "moon." We call this period "adapting" and it refers to the first year or two after "the honey". We will discuss the various differences between the way we adapted forty years ago and what the issues are now. We didn't even think of adjusting in our first marriage. We were in love and we assumed everything would fall into place. We never thought about problems.

At 60 plus, we know that all relationships have problems. We admit our mistakes and hope that our experience allows us a smoother transition into our new state. Couples, afraid of repeating their mistakes and not willing to allow time for adapting, will probably stay in a limited relationship. They will not give up their primary residences but will continue in a monogamous, sexual commitment. They are often at one place or the other and are living what is essentially a twenty-four hour date.

Minor aggravations can become major problems in adapting to each other. We are now set in our ways and fully convinced that each has the best answer. Habits we bring with us are unimportant unless they lead to conflict between the two parties. This usually occurs only when simple routines are carried to extreme. Whether we are night or day people, can affect so many of our daily routines. When do we go to bed? Are we both early risers? Do we work better in the morning or the late evening? When do we like to eat? Besides time schedules that can differ, there are other potential aggravations that need to be smoothed over after "the honey" time. Do we have the same taste in food? Is breakfast only coffee? Do we both drink alcohol? Do we have a cocktail time? Do we need times apart during the day for our own projects? Are we willing to share household chores? What do we do with previous spouse's pictures and memorabilia? Do we display any?

Is one an outdoors person and more interested in sports? If so, does he or she prefer outdoor activities of any kind in nice weather. Walking, gardening, sitting outside and sports such as golf and tennis at this age are all appealing to this type of person. If the other partner in a new relationship has little or no interest in these activities, they will find that they do very little together. This may not bother all, but totally different activities create different social groups, and the relationship will have difficulty growing. *While time alone to do your own thing is good, no time together is like being single or alone again.* Sports that are known to one party can be shared with the other. Someone who has never skied could be tempted to go with their partner on a learn-to ski vacation. Peggy was introduced to her first week of skiing last year. Similarly, tennis and golf can be taken up at any age and become part of a couple's new social life. Dancing, particularly country western and "fifties" style dancing, has become extremely popular these days. We enjoy it more and usually do the steps better than younger couples. Others at this age enjoy less strenuous activities but still have the opportunity to either learn something new with their partner or share a common interest. Bridge, reading, photography, music and art are quieter activities that can be shared.

The adapting period can also uncover some differences that were somewhat glossed over in the initial months of a relationship. These are more attitudes than habits and they have usually been with us for a long time. They don't have to be logical and for this reason they are much more difficult to handle. This is part of the baggage that we bring with us which we have been packing all our lives.

During courtship, most couples eat out more frequently and at better restaurants than at another time. It's a social time for both that is filled with excitement and memories. After "the honey", eating out patterns usually change. A frugal nature of one of the partners may surface at this time and restaurants are now chosen by entertainment coupons or "2-fors". It is at this time that carry-out becomes the restaurant of the evening. More eating is done at home, which is considerably less expensive, than during the courtship period. This is an accepted pattern for many but for some, it could cause a problem.

Vacations and travel are almost an expected way of life in the 60's plus age group. The cost of vacations and travel are often determined by the amount of money each partner is willing to spend. Again, it's sometimes more an attitude than the availability of the money itself. Some people compare all vacation costs to a vacation they can take with the car, camping or to close-by "old haunts". If the costs exceed this, they balk at going. The ability to travel by car will depend upon a couple's eyesight and reflexes that decrease with age. It's a desirable, cheaper and often relaxing way to travel as long as driving is physically possible and it's what both like to do. Cruises are extremely popular and almost every couple plan at least one.

If the couple have settled into one residence, married or unmarried, the question of home improvements will surely surface quickly. The idea of making the house decor "theirs", appeals to both----the cost may not. Both have definite ideas and tastes that may conflict. Some men may have lost interest in house style or left it to a previous partner. Women like to nest but generally like to beautify their homes with stylish changes from time to time. They are usually more aware of design innovations that might lead to costly enlargements, new color schemes and bed and bathroom refinements. While we have been used to small bathrooms and very practical kitchens, today's designs are making models of the 50's and 60's look outdated. Creating contemporary designs will largely depend upon where the couple have chosen to reside, who owns the house, whether they are legally married and most importantly, the amount of money each party is willing to spend on the improvement. If one party agrees to only minimal renovation, compromise is needed or trouble begins. If the house belongs to only one individual, the other may be reluctant to invest in a property that could be short lived. Death, infirmity or separation could mean relocation and the sale of the property in a shorter than expected time. Proceeds from the sale would belong to the legal owner. Major structural changes are very expensive, disrupt daily routines and are generally stressful with multiple design modifications. For these reasons, new couples should discuss thoroughly and plan ahead to make the renovation period as smooth as possible. While all these housing factors have undoubtedly been discussed during "the honey", often no real decisions were made and serious discussions usually start much later.

We would be remiss if we did not point out that *everybody has at least one frugal "quirk" in their soul.* This is not an age related thing but definitely gets worse with age. These "quirks" are often not recognized as an annoyance in the early stages of a relationship but become more pronounced with time. Healthy people in their 60's often have a sensitive area of spending. They may have been able to adjust to increasing prices over the years but one area will be their "frugal quirk." These can range from leaving a tip acceptable thirty years ago, calling clothing prices outrageous, keeping a car way beyond its' expected life and generally comparing today's prices with those in their earlier years. It's usually one thing or one area that causes them grief. While they are alone, they don't think of it as a problem. In a relationship, it can be a problem for the new partner after "the honey".

Chapter 6

Legal Problems and Some Solutions

Since love does not conquer all, the new couple, married or unmarried, must deal with financially supporting their relationship while each preserves their own assets. Besides the basic living expenses, there are financial issues that will affect them now as well as in the future. These issues may decide whether the couple becomes legally married or not. We are not lawyers and do not intend to cover all the possibilities that couples could encounter. Here are some of the most important issues with some solutions.

Prenuptial Agreements

Prenuptial agreements, which are signed by both parties, are drawn up after separate consultation with lawyers for each party. One lawyer cannot represent both parties unless a waiver is obtained from both. Individuals in a prenuptial agreement are considered adverse parties with divergent interests. The completed, signed document can eliminate financial problems of asset ownership and management and ease the minds of the future inheritors. These agreements can cover anything the couple might foresee as financial difficulties in their future. The prenuptial agreement deals with the assets each person brings to the marriage and establishes the ownership of all property real or otherwise. It lists or names all possessions which remain in the control of one of the parties. Homes, cars, stocks, bonds, commercial properties, boats and planes are part of this group. It may also include furniture, pictures and jewelry. "Prenups", as they are called, can also include financial arrangements to be followed after the marriage has been performed. As an example, it can stipulate a certain percentage each party is to contribute toward the household budget, mortgage, entertainment, insurance, and long term care each month or year as written. These agreements should provide clear instructions regarding residence rights for a surviving spouse, particularly if the deceased is the sole owner of their residence. Provisions for the surviving spouse in this case should be covered in both the last will and testament and the prenuptial agreement. We have covered it in more detail under the section below. Prenuptial agreements do not limit either party from giving any of their assets to the other as either gifts, bequests or establishing joint ownership of property previously owned by one, any time during their marriage. As an example, money in a bank account listed in the "prenup" of one party can be easily transferred to the other anytime after the marriage.

Prenuptial agreements are intended for those planning marriage but documents,called contracts, can be drafted and signed by both parties who merely cohabitate. It is important to realize that a contract is between two living individuals and if one partner dies, the will of the deceased takes over. Therefore, since the contract is no longer valid, any important agreements between the two parties, should be listed in their will as well as in the contract. Couples living together usually leave their assets in their own name. They may draft an agreement on the handling of expenses and the ownership of property, such as furniture brought to the mutual residence and used while living together. They can put anything into this document that they want, but most couples living together don't bother. To reiterate, contracts terminate at death and the will takes over. A contract helps when couples split-up but if one dies, it has no power.

Unmarried couples usually operate on a month to month basis, dividing all expenses as mutually agreed. They can pool their moneys equally for social events, dining out or traveling, with one person taking charge of paying the bills. They can do this by having a "social wallet" where their equal contributions are used until exhausted. There are many variations of this and each couple can make up their own money arrangement.

Regardless of the sharing of the month to month expenses, either party of a non-legal couple can separate themselves from their partner at any time with minimal complications. As the law reads now, there is no legal commitment to provide for each other in either daily routine expenses or more serious life traumas such as a significant heart attack, stroke or cancer. A non-legal partner does not have to be involved with the expenses of a long term care facility but should have a moral obligation to give emotional support. If the ailing person cannot function on their own, the family of the stricken person might have to assume all financial obligations until Medicaid requirements are met. The healthy one, if he or she is so inclined, can stroll into the sunset looking for a new, *healthy* partner.

Wills

Wills are for everybody and everybody should have one, whether they are married or just living together. Wills direct the distribution of assets following the death of an individual. They specify bequests of tangible property including house (s) and all household effects, jewelry, cars and everything else owned outright by the deceased. These bequests can be made to family members, friends or institutions. If they intend to exclude any immediate family, they should have a lawyer draft the will. Individuals living together have no legal recourse if left out of their partner's will but a legal wife does have rights. Most states have automatic inheritance laws for married couples but not those living together. A legal wife has survivor benefits that vary from state to state according to community property laws. Although assets can be designated to anyone in a will, legal documents are always necessary. After a couple is married, everything acquired after that day becomes joint property, unless otherwise stipulated in their prenuptial agreement. Couples living together can leave assets to one another but these can be contested by immediate family members. Bequests to a surviving partner should be specified in the will with a hope that the family will not contest it.

In setting up a will, samples are available in any public library. These samples are probably best used for small estates with few bequests. Any complicated distribution of assets is better handled by a lawyer. An executor is designated in a will. This person must follow the wishes of the deceased and receives as payment, a percentage of the estate. He is responsible for carrying out all burial wishes and for paying all debts, taxes, medical and funeral expenses of the deceased. The executor does not have to be related to the deceased but usually works closely with the family lawyer.

Within a will, several trusts may be established. These can deal with children or grandchildren of the deceased who are designated in the will to inherit but are presently below the age specified by the deceased. Many believe that those under the age of twenty-five or thirty, are not mature enough to deal with an inheritance. An important issue in any will involving a married or unmarried couple living in a home owned by only one of the partners, is a provision specifying continued residence of the surviving partner. This can be established by putting the home with its contents in a trust for the inheritors. This holds the property for the inheritors of the deceased but allows the surviving spouse or partner to continue to live at the residence. Provisions can stipulate that remarriage or cohabitation of a surviving partner would dissolve all residence rights. It can also stipulate that the property must be used as the primary residence of the surviving partner or spouse. Failure to provide proper maintenance of the property and prompt payment of all bills can also void the trust. The trust is terminated upon the death of the surviving spouse or partner. All these and any other stipulations can be clearly defined in the trust for the benefit of the surviving spouse or significant other.

Another important point to be considered is the formation of a trust for the eventual heirs with the surviving partner as the trustee. The advantage of this kind of a trust is that the income from the trust is available to be distributed to the heirs in limited amounts. This is taxable income but usually at a lower bracket. The income and the assets may be distributed to the heirs as desired or retained in trust till the death of the trustee, which dissolves the trust.

Stock that has accumulated significant taxable capital gains may be transferred to a legal spouse prior to death and the purchase price is then considered to be the price at the time of transfer. As an example, if one had purchased Exxon at $10.00 a share and the market price at the time of transfer was 150.00, the purchase price would now be considered $150.00 and the capital gains from the original purchase would be wiped out. This can only be done between legal spouses and before death.

Power of Attorney

The Power of Attorney, like a will, is a legal document giving authority to a designated individual, who does not have to be either a lawyer or a relative, to act for that person in financial and legal matters. This would include such things as bank withdrawals, signing of contracts, appearing on your behalf and to sell, assign or transfer any real or personal property. The designated individual may invest and reinvest all assets or property as he wishes. He may also give consent for medical or surgical procedures, if not contrary to the patient's advance medical directive, as well as employ attorneys, investment counsel, doctors and nurses. Because of this unlimited power given to another person, one should designate this power with extreme caution. The wrong individual with a Power of Attorney can wipe out an individual's assets in a very short time. It should be noted that a "durable" power of attorney (DPOA) gives broad powers to a designated person and remains in force even if the individual becomes incapacitated. A general Power of Attorney (POA) expires when one becomes incapacitated.

Living Will and Medical Decision Power of Attorney (Advance Medical Directive)

These documents are equally as important as any of the above. People our age eventually will have health care decisions that they may not be able to make themselves. The living will states the wishes of an individual concerning the extent of his medical treatment at the time of a life threatening situation. The living will allows an individual to receive only the treatment he would have chosen himself. This directive usually asks that no life support mechanisms be used. Contrary to the living will, the Medical Power of Attorney designates another individual to make a medical decision for him when the person is incapable of making an informed decision. With this directive, one may withhold or withdraw life prolonging procedures that are not specified in the living will. It can also ask that medicines, nourishment, and supportive devices be administered solely to eliminate and relieve pain and not to delay death. The directive can state that we do not want any of our resources to be exhausted in the vain struggle to keep us breathing nor the energy and emotions of our family to be drained away in a futile vigil. Both the living will and a medical power of attorney can be combined into a single document.

The absence of a living will or a medical directive can cause unneeded anguish and stress at the time of a medical emergency. Although the spouse or the next of kin is the legal spokesperson for the patient, he or she could be overruled by the patient's doctors in a near death situation. If the patient cannot communicate his wishes and does not have these documents, the doctors are bound to utilize all means to extend life, even if the next of kin objects.

There are some non-emotional reasons that prompt some couples to take the plunge and get married at our age. Unmarried partners cannot be included in their companion's medical insurance since they are not a legal family member. Downsizing has caused many people their jobs and their company's health insurance plan. A married individual who has lost his health plan may piggyback onto his spouse's medical insurance that is considerably cheaper than paying for an individual plan. In addition, an unmarried partner cannot legally make medical decisions for the other unless they are designated in a legal medical power of attorney. As we have already stated, most unmarried couples do not bother drafting such legal documents. This means that the gravely ill party must depend upon his children to make these decisions, excluding the loving partner. Often couples are far away from their families so that their children must make decisions sometimes based on inadequate information and often by phone or fax. Although technical communications are much better between both individuals and medical institutions, they will always lack the emotional closeness that family members or loving partners can add in a traumatic health crisis.

Chapter 7

Aging Gracefully----Go Ahead and Try

We all hope to age with style, vigor and a full deck upstairs, but this does not always happen. Our aging starts at birth and is the product of our years, our environment, the genes we were born with and the good and bad habits that we picked up along the way. In this chapter we would like to discuss the physical changes that may occur in our aging bodies. In the next chapter, we will talk about some of the mental diseases that can take over our minds. Men and women this age are more sensitive, knowledgeable and also cautious about the aging process.

As this book deals with relationships of those over 60, we would first like to discuss some of the physical difficulties that may prevent a relationship from getting off the ground. These conditions can also occur much later in a relationship or marriage but may not present the same problems then as they would in the beginning of a relationship. People at our age are nervous and perhaps cautious about first encounters with the opposite sex and if they have a physical limitation, they may be very wary about becoming involved.

Urinary incontinence in either party would probably be on the top of the list of conditions discouraging the beginning of a new relationship. This condition is best defined as the uncontrolled loss of urine. One out of twenty-five Americans or almost ten million people, have urinary incontinence. It can affect people at any age but is especially common in women over the age of 65. Loss of bladder control is not a disease itself but is the result of muscle damage from pregnancy, infections, injury or one of several other conditions. There are different types of incontinence. Stress, urge and mixed incontinence account for about 80% of all cases. Stress incontinence is the most common and accounts for 65% of all incontinence. It is the loss of urine due to the sudden rise of pressure in the abdomen It is not related to psychological stress. Simple, physical movements such as dancing, sneezing, coughing, jogging and lifting can cause stress incontinence. Urge incontinence is the loss of urine at an inappropriate time because the voiding reflex, which is a signal indicating the bladder is full, is out of control. Mixed incontinence is some combination of the two. Alcohol, caffeine and some medications can make the problems of incontinence worse. With the growing number of treatments now available, 85-90% of all stress incontinence can be treated. Even though this condition is more common in the elderly, bladder control problems are not a natural part of aging. Surgeries for cancer of the prostate or surgery for prostatic enlargement are the most common causes of incontinence in men.

If either party in a new relationship suffers from this condition, it is quite likely that they would not pursue any type of intimate contact. The embarrassment of their condition would hinder the progress of a new couple's relationship. This is a shame because people with this problem have in recent years found a community of equally effected individuals, and treatments have become available. Frequent articles in popular magazines discuss the problem and make it easier for both men and women to talk about it openly.

Other pre-existing major illnesses and the consequences of their treatment can create a barrier to beginning couples in this age group. By this, we are referring to conditions such as strokes, heart disease, and cancer. Even though these may have been successfully treated or arrested, they are still a part of a person's medical history that they bring to the new relationship. **Cancer of the breast,** treated by mastectomy, often leaves a woman reluctant to engage in any new intimate relations. Lumpectomy was not the treatment of choice by many doctors only fifteen to twenty years ago. Therefore mature, senior women who suffered with breast cancer, usually had a radical or a modified radical mastectomy rather than a lumpectomy. Women often felt mentally and physically scarred by the procedure, had few role models who would talk about it and much less support than is present in today's society. Silicone implants had their start with the women in this group. Even with adequate support, older women may not feel as comfortable as some of the younger women who now undergo lumpectomies for the same type of cancer. **Radical prostatectomy** (removal of the entire prostate) for cancer can have a similar, though not as visible, effect on men as mastectomy has on women. The procedure can leave a man both incontinent and impotent because of nerve damage that is hard to avoid even in the hands of the best surgeon. For obvious reasons, just mentioned, males with these complications are exceedingly reluctant to date. The history of cancer anywhere in the body, whether arrested or not, can be a threat to a new relationship. Any type of active cancer in a male or a female makes an individual reluctant to enter into a potentially long term affair.

Heart disease, because it is so treatable, is not looked upon in the same light as cancer. Those with heart disease often impose limitations on themselves that are greater than they need. Individuals with coronary artery disease (CAD) are often reluctant to engage in sexual activities because of fear of having a heart attack during sex. This is especially common with men who have bypass surgery who are initially extremely cautious about having sex. Articles in the medical literature should alleviate these fears. It was found that the only group that had a high risk were those that had sex with an illicit partner. For those in a committed relationship, the risk is minimal and probably no greater than mowing the lawn.

The after effects of a **stroke** can be far more devastating to a new couple than a heart attack. These effects are often very visible and recognizable. If there is permanent paralysis, movement and the ability to perform the tasks of daily living are compromised. The effects of strokes can change one's life style because the victim becomes more dependent on others. Driving privileges may be lost and require the individual to relocate. Strokes attack the brain and can limit speech as well as other brain functions. Fortunately, not all strokes leave permanent damage. Some are mild with almost complete recovery and require no changes in life style or habits.

A variety of progressive, neurological diseases such as **Parkinson's disease** often appear at this age and severely limit a person's movements. At this point, medicine has not come up with a cure and such individuals gradually become incapacitated.

Body Changes No One Looks Forward To

Everything eventually wears out----but fortunately, not all at the same time. Some people are in an apparent "time freeze" of physical and mental health while others go "downhill" one organ at a time. Those in the "time freeze" are rare, have good genes and sometimes lie. We will deal mainly with changes that happen to the "downhill gang". These changes may come whether you are in a relationship,

78

just starting one or hoping to start one. Those lucky enough to be in a relationship, married or not, hopefully will have the advantage of the best support system in their declining years.

The most obvious changes of aging appear in the **skin.** There are three common skin changes that happen with age. As we age, skin loses its' elasticity, gravity takes over, and wrinkles and sagging skin begin to appear. Brown aging-spots due to accumulation of melanin is the second skin change and small, subcutaneous hemorrhages, because of fragile capillaries, are the third tell-tale sign of a person's age. In the last ten years it has become accepted that the worst culprit in causing wrinkles is excessive exposure to the sun. Now they tell us! The sun has also been implicated in the rising frequency of cancer of the skin, including melanoma, which is more frequent in light skinned, sun-exposed individuals. We seniors seem to follow the sun for year round warmth and may be exposing our bodies to twelve months of strong exposure to the sun rather than the three months that we used to have. Healthy habits for healthier skin include: drinking lots of water, not smoking, getting sufficient sleep, gentle cleansing habits, exercise and maintaining a constant, good weight. People that fluctuate in weight due to dieting often have more wrinkles. Avoiding sunlight is the healthiest habit you can develop for protecting your skin. There is no good tan unless it comes out of a bottle. All individuals should avoid peak exposure times between 10:00am to 2:00pm and wear protective sun screens up to at least 15 SPF. Some medications, for example Tylenol, make some skin more sensitive to the sun and therefore all instructions should be carefully read. Cosmetic creams containing retinol are readily available now and have proven to be somewhat beneficial in reducing wrinkles. Injections of botulism toxin (Botox) can improve wrinkles but only temporarily and the injections must be repeated every few months. A face tuck is probably preferential and definitely, if successful, is more permanent.

Hair today----gone tomorrow. Hair loss in men can start as early as the teenage years but usually starts after middle age. Most men have what is referred to as male pattern baldness which is genetically passed down from parents or grandparents on either side. The cause is unknown and until recently untreatable until the advent of minoxidil. Most men over 60 have at least a thinning of their hair if not an actual bald area. As females age, their hair thins to the point where bald spots may develop but not as much and not in the same pattern as males. Post-menopausal hair thinning is common all over the body for women but males seem to suffer less body hair thinning than women as they age. Hair loss often follows chemotherapy and radiation in both men and women but the hair usually grows back after treatment is stopped and is often a different color and texture. Other reasons for hair loss are stress, medications (even aspirin), surgery and hair coloring abuse. Wigs and hair pieces can be a great help in any of these stressful situations. A person's original hair color, whether male or female, left untouched, will lose its' color and eventually become gray. The time it takes will vary tremendously from person to person and the eventual shade of gray is just as variable. This is due to loss of melanin pigment in the hair shaft.

Almost all older individuals have significant changes that take place in their **eyes, teeth** and **hearing ability.** Just about everyone between the ages of 40 - 50, uses some type of corrective lens and the condition usually continues to worsen with age. It is rare to find someone over 60 without glasses or contact lenses. Recent laser surgery on the cornea has drastically begun to change the need for glasses or contacts. What is very common as we age, is the formation of cataracts. Cataracts are the clouding of the lens in one or both eyes. Doctors are not sure of the cause but, fortunately, most are correctable by surgical techniques. Other old age eye problems that we would just as soon skip include macular degeneration and glaucoma. Macular degeneration is damage to the macula which is the central part of the retina and results in a blind spot in the middle of the visual field. Laser surgery has been used but not always successfully. Recently, the FDA approved a drug that may slow the progression of this disease. Glaucoma is an increased pressure in the eye that potentially can lead to blindness if not treated.

A set of **teeth** in a glass, on a nightstand beside a bed, won't contribute to the romance of a relationship. For some people, a complete set of dentures is reason enough to go slowly into a lasting partnership. Of course, if both parties have dentures, it may be a perfect match. At this age, teeth are usually lost to gum disease (a very treatable condition) rather than cavities. Most people in their 60's have at least one permanent bridge. The technology of filling is somewhat different today than many years ago. Dentists in our youth were taught to drill out large amounts of a decayed tooth to be sure of getting all the decay. Because of this, older teeth have huge fillings, thin walls and therefore, often chip or break more easily. Now, dentists, with better instruments, take less of the tooth around the decayed area and leave the tooth stronger. Older teeth also become discolored particularly in smokers and those that have chewed tobacco. Older men and women, especially in their eighties, do not brush as well as they used to because of lack of strength, desire, patience and forgetfulness. As a result, the gums recede and the roots become exposed. Cosmetic dentistry has become more and more important to a larger group of people other than entertainers. Teeth whitening, straightening and implants are increasingly more popular.

The sensitivity of taste buds decreases with age and more so in some people than others. The ability to enjoy food, therefore, decreases as we age. The taste buds that remain will dictate our favorite foods.

Hearing loss is very common after the age of 60 and most people should expect to lose their ability to hear the very high and moderate-to-low frequencies of human speech. Most hearing loss is due to heredity or the continued exposure to very loud noises. Hearing aides are getting smaller, better and less conspicuous now, making them more acceptable to the hearing impaired. For some reason we do not mind wearing glasses at any age but the idea of using a hearing aide signals old age. We may definitely need them but we'll put off the purchase 'till we can hardly carry on a conversation. We will still blame others for our poor hearing and continue to say, "Why don't you speak up?"

Arthritis is an "inflammation" of a joint and is a growing problem due to the increased numbers of the aging population. There are two main types of arthritis: osteoarthritis and rheumatoid arthritis. **Osteoarthritis** is a degeneration of cartilage between the ends of bones and causes stiffness or pain in the hands, spine, or knees. There are probably 17 million Americans that suffer from this and almost all are over the age of 45. To a certain extent, most people over the age of 60 have some degree of osteoarthritis, many with no symptoms. Overweight individuals who do not exercise are more prone to develop this type of arthritis. People, such as athletes, who frequently injure joints are more lightly to develop osteoarthritis in the traumatized joint in later years. The other significant type of arthritis is **rheumatoid arthritis.** Over two million people in the United States suffer from this type of arthritis and two thirds of these are women. Rheumatoid arthritis is a disease of the immune system of unknown cause and usually effects individuals between forty and sixty but can be found in some children and young women. Most people with arthritis can be helped with anti-inflammatory medications such as aspirin and other over the counter medications. It is probably prudent for someone with rheumatoid arthritis to be under the care of a physician. Either type of arthritis can be a hardship for those in or developing a new relationship. The pain is often intense and the condition can decrease the person's ability and desire for activity. The healthy partner cannot help being moved with compassion but patience can grow thin in any type of relationship.

Replacement parts for our damaged joints have kept many seniors on the tennis courts and golf courses longer than they ever expected. Hip and knee replacements are slowly becoming as common as replacing any worn-out part in a machine. Replacement parts, and the surgical techniques to install them, have become more accepted by the general public and the medical profession. We can now replace the lens of the eye, parts of the hearing apparatus, teeth and heart valves. It's probably one of the reasons why Medicare is going broke.

"Oh, my aching back" can be heard at every senior gathering. **Back pain** is the most frequent reason that older individuals visit their doctor. It can be due to osteoarthritis, the discs between the vertebra and not infrequently various muscle pulls or strains. Treatment is often difficult or only temporarily successful. Many individuals suffer with chronic back pain which can be somewhat relieved by aspirin and other similar medications. Back x-rays most often show signs of osteoarthritis in seniors who have no symptoms. However, if told of the x-ray findings, they will probably develop some symptoms. A recent study showed that most back pain would disappear within six months *without any surgery.*

Osteoporosis is a problem that effects many more women than men. These women are post-menopausal and hence the term "dowager's hump." Rapid bone loss after menopause causes bone thinning. Bones of the wrist, hips and spine become brittle and fracture easily. It is estimated that as many as 40% of women over the age of 50 will have a broken bone related to osteoporosis. In addition to the menopause, other risk factors for osteoporosis are: Caucasian or Asian descent, thin or small build, smoking, drinking too much alcohol, lack of exercise and family history. This disease can be evaluated by a physician in conjunction with bone density testing. A certain amount of prevention can be achieved by taking adequate calcium and being involved in weight bearing exercise such as tennis, running and regular walking. Over the last years, hormone replacement therapy has been the most talked about and yet controversial treatment for osteoporosis. Recent FDA rulings have allowed new drug combinations which appear to decrease the risks of cancer of the uterus which was always the biggest drawback for hormone replacement therapy.

Foot aches and pains are prevalent at this age but are more frequent in women than in men. They are not necessarily age related but occur in women who have worn fashionable shoe styles with pointed toes, platforms and stiletto heels. Women often developed bunions and hammer toes which caused considerable pain. Women whose jobs required them to stand for long hours such as sales people, waitresses and assembly line workers are much more prone to develop foot ailments. Surgery is about the only way to really correct such problems but because the recovery time is long, most avoid this remedy as long as they can. Women of all ages today are avoiding foot problems by using more sensible shoes and reserving fashion shoes for their nights out. Walking to and from work in tennis shoes is now a common sight.

Two common problems in old age are **constipation** and **gas**. Everyone gets gas. Much of the gas is caused by swallowed air. The gas that is not caused by swallowed air is due to the breakdown of foods in the gastrointestinal tract. Foods containing large quantities of complex carbohydrates, like beans and broccoli, produce more gas. Many individuals are lactose intolerant after the age of 40 and produce gas because of the milk they drink. The gastrointestinal tract appears to slow down in older individuals leading to constipation. Part of this may be due to inactivity and a poor diet. People over 60 who do regular exercise, drink 8 - 10 glasses of water a day and eat foods containing adequate fiber, are rarely constipated. Many medications taken by seniors, such as diuretics, pain killers, and even antihistamines, can also cause constipation. The high incidence of constipation coincides with the high incidence of **diverticulosis** in this population. Diverticulosis is the formation of small pouches, especially in the lower part of the large intestine. These can fill with feces and become infected leading to diverticulitis.

Heartburn, now referred to as Reflux Esophogitis, has become the newest popular disease and is popping up more frequently than new internet companies. Many medicines are now directed towards curing this new epidemic and these are actively being pushed by drug companies. Half the people at any social gathering will tell you that they are sufferers of "Reflux".

Pot Bellies are not exclusive to men. They are considered to be part and parcel of beer drinking, snacking and watching football on TV. Since more men seem to fall into this category, we think of men as having "pots". Women, however, can also have pot bellies due to their role as child bearers, cooks that taste, and having had little or no time for exercise during most of their life. Women of our generation were never encouraged to exercise as adults but were often encouraged to drink lots of beer, whole milk and other fattening foods. Proper posture is the best over all cover-up for a protruding abdomen. This applies to both men and women. Even those that are heavy will look better and younger when they are standing tall and holding in their stomachs.

These diseases and changes in individuals over 60 can have a significant effect on starting or maintaining any type of relationship. Dating is easier and more satisfying when you are healthy.

When It Doesn't Get Any Better

Most people are not lucky enough to die in their sleep without any serious ailments. *Anything can happen to anyone at anytime*. We should have a plan for the "what if" days. We do not have to invest a lot of money or be obsessed with the planning, but we should have some idea before something major happens. We have discussed the legal issues of sickness and death in the previous chapter but now let's look at some of the physical changes that may be necessary in our living environment.

What if we suddenly can't drive? How do we get food and make all of our appointments? What if we need a walker or a wheel chair? Is our home able to accommodate these changes? Do we need wider doors, ramps, rails, better lighting and a bedroom with bath on the first floor. Do we need to move? Is it time for assisted living or a nursing home? Will our partner come with us? Am I going to be alone?

Prior to arriving at this stage in your life, serious thought should have been given to the financial side of your last years. Medicare does not cover assisted living or nursing home care except for a short term rehabilitation. Most supplemental insurances are written with the same restrictions. Since the average stay in a nursing home is two and a half years, it is possible to exhaust your entire life savings in that time. As it is estimated that between 25 percent and 50 percent of people over age 65 will need nursing home care, it is prudent to look into long term care insurance as we discussed previously. It's costly but worth looking into as assurance of good care while leaving something for one's children. Every senior's haunting fear is that of being a burden to his or her children.

If a couple is unmarried, what do they do at this point in their lives? They have no legal obligation to their partner to support them when one of them becomes handicapped. As we have stated, they certainly should have a moral obligation to emotionally support their companion. This is particularly true if they have been in a relationship for many years. However, the unmarried partner cannot be faulted for letting the family takeover. The true strength of the relationship would become evident at this time.

There is tremendous emotional involvement for the healthy partner in caring for the other. It's physically and emotionally stressful twenty-four hours a day. Because of this, it's not unusual for one of an elderly couple to die and the remaining partner to die shortly after. It was reported that survivors are 63 percent more likely to die within four years than other spouses who were not caregivers. In addition, they have higher levels of depression and often do not have enough time themselves for exercise, rest or even seeing a physician when they are not feeling well.

Chapter 8

Mind Games You Don't Want to Play

Everyone over 60 has some degree of *short term memory loss*. If you do not think so, get a group of your peers together, tell them about your most recent memory lapse and listen as each one tells you an even better story of theirs. We recently did this by chance and found that the entire group over the last six weeks had experienced some episode of short term memory loss. They were not embarrassed to tell their stories but were rather comforted by everyone else's revelations. These instances can happen once a day, once a week or once a month and apparently have no pattern or relation to each other. One time we can forget what we went to the store for and another time, we can forget the name of our best friend or someone we played golf with for thirty years. Nobody seems to know what causes these lapses but drug companies are working furiously to come up with a pill to prevent the process. Memory loss may be due to chemical depletion in old age, decreased blood supply and effects of medication or possibly stress and other emotional problems. Although one of the prime symptoms of Alzheimer's disease is memory loss, the episodes referred to above are not necessarily the beginnings of Alzheimer's disease. They may be part of what we are at 60 plus. Not everyone is effected.

Alzheimer's disease is a form of dementia that is irreversible and is characterized by a slow but steady destruction of areas of the brain that control memory and reasoning. Most health professionals agree that there are at least three stages of the disease and that they often overlap. The first stage, which usually lasts two to four years, includes recent memory loss, confusion about places, lose of both initiative and zest for life. At this time, mood and personality changes begin to take place and individuals may make bad decisions. During this first stage, Alzheimer victims may have trouble handling money, paying bills and take longer with routine chores. Bills may be paid more than once or not paid at all, items are lost and phone numbers and names cannot be remembered. Stage two is considered the longest stage and can last up to ten years. During this time, memory loss and confusion increase and the attention span decreases. Family members and friends are not always recognized and repetitive physical movements become obvious. Problems arise with reading, writing and numbers and they often make up stories if they cannot remember the facts. They sometimes become sloppy, stop bathing and have trouble getting dressed. They may see or hear things that are not real and later in this stage, need full time supervision. At this stage they become suspicious, sleep often and may have huge appetites but cannot remember when they last ate. The third and final stage, which usually lasts from one to three years, finds the patient with little capacity for self care. They cannot recognize family members or themselves in a mirror. They can no longer communicate and often lose both bowel and bladder control. The disease is presently considered untreatable, although, recently it has been suggested that hormone replacement therapy in women and doses of nicotine in both sexes may be able to slow the progression. Recently, researchers isolated a long sought-after enzyme that is thought to be critical in the development of this disease. It is hoped that medications can be developed that will counteract the effects of this enzyme and prevent or slow the progress of this terrible affliction.

Depression is seen frequently in the elderly, especially in women. This is not necessarily due to the larger number of women in this age group but is possibly related to hormones or to the fact that women have more depressing events in their lives than men. Maybe, they just react to these events differently than men. It is not a disease of the aged exclusively but there are many in this group who are faced with life's serious problems and are more subject to periodic mild to moderate bouts of depression. A feeling of hopelessness with the present and no desire to do anything special in the future, as well as a lack of zest for living are the hallmarks of depression. Some people can be periodically and slightly depressed while others can be so depressed that they are almost unable to move from their bed or write their name. Individuals can sit for hours and hours in a chair and just stare into space and not say a word. A number of prescription medications have been introduced in the last few years that can do wonders for people with depression. The number of people on these medications, including Prozac, has so dramatically increased that they have replaced the drug of the 1960's, Valium, as the most over-prescribed drug in this country.

Obsessive behavior is another manifestation of growing older. It appears that one of the most common compulsions is the obsession with money and personal belongings. It can be quite irrational, difficult to deal with and enough to drive surrounding family and friends into periodic seclusion. Although, this is very noticeable in the entire geriatric population, it is most striking in patients confined to nursing homes and assisted living facilities. They feel that family and personnel involved in their care are stealing or attempting to steal their money and valuables. Patients with Alzheimer's disease often hide their money and small possessions in secret places around them and because of their memory loss, instantly forget where they hid them. This reinforces their belief that someone is stealing from them. It's an unending cycle. These same people cannot understand where their savings have gone. With increased memory loss, they have no concept of present day prices for goods and services. They become totally unrealistic and incapable of comprehending logical reasoning.

Eccentricities of the Aging Brain

Apart from the major diseases of both mind and body, we have found seniors to be a pretty funny bunch. We think we act with great wisdom, but are often out of date, do not understand and don't want to accept the world as it is today. We like the way things were and don't see why they had to change. We were talking with a friend who could not understand why football rules and style of playing had to change from the way it was in the 1940's. Others don't understand why we have to pay so much for cars and food now or why our children feel that they have to have bigger homes and "everything" before they reach thirty. Even though we are generally conservative and somewhat resistant to change, we would definitely *not* like to return to the era of telephone party lines, families with one car, no TV, no answering machines, no frozen dinners or convenient shopping malls. We selectively accept the new technologies that we can easily understand and use in our daily lives. We are not concerned with the global picture until we see resolution of national problems. In our younger years, a dinner out was just the two of us. Now, it's fast food for the whole family. Although we see the necessity of this, we still remember candlelight dinners for two.

In closing this chapter, we would like to list some of the every day *minor irritations* to ourselves and those around us, many of which are related to our aging brains.

1. When did Seniors become so pushy?
2. *Seniors' motto.* If it's free, we'll take it!
3. Why can't a remote have just ON/OFF, UP/DOWN and LOUD/SOFT!
4. Why is everything "self serve"?
5. Who needs an ATM? I always carry cash.
6. When was Tums replaced by prescription medication?
7. Does everyone need a cellular phone and a car phone?
8. No matter how many pairs of glasses I have, I'm always looking for one.
9. Seniors drive even slower than the speed limit!
10. What do I need E Mail for? My friends don't use computers.
11. I only eat at restaurants that have an "early bird" special! Two for one is even better!
12. What's a digital TV?
13. Too many grandchildren----I get their names all mixed up.
14. Did I take my medications? Is the glass wet?
15. Why call a repairman---maybe my son can fix it!
16. Who's going to drive? Can he drive after dark?
17. Haven't you ever lost your car in the parking lot?
18. I'm freezing----who turned down the heat?
19. Can't do that----that's my nap time!
20. The "boys" now meet in the morning at the "golden arches".

21. Doesn't anyone eat beef anymore?
22. Telephones are too automated----I want to speak to a real person.
23. The shoe department is the only place you can find to sit down in a large department store these days.
24. You become intolerant of people who are intolerant.
25. Rather than for romantic reasons, you turn out the lights to save money.
26. I can't make it----this is my weekend to baby-sit the grandkids.
27. Can't baby-sit----I've got a date!

Humor that has circulated on the internet, has come up with the following signs indicating that you are already old or almost there.

----Your little black book contains only names that end in M.D.
----Everything hurts, and what doesn't hurt, doesn't work!
----Your back goes out more often than you do.
----You join a health club but don't go.
----You look forward to a dull evening.
----Your knees buckle but your belt won't.
----You begin to regret all those times you resisted temptation.
----The little old lady you helped across the street, looks pretty good to you!

If people look old--do they act old? No, not necessarily but often a physical ailment in someone over 60 translates into old or presents an old image. The prime factor affecting one's attitude about age and aging is their **mindset**. Major medical problems can alter this mindset and be a detriment to a vital outlook. If one's health is reasonably good, a lethargic mind set about being over 60 can be reconditioned, *especially if a new relationship emerges.*

Curiosity is definitely an advantage. Curiosity is the willingness to expand into new horizons and explore new interests, hobbies and people. This may be easier for a woman who has been a homemaker with a limited career. She may have started expanding when her children started middle school and became more independent. At 60, she has already had a head start in finding new friends, new activities and new interests. The male must continue to work and support the family through the children's college years. Because of this, he gets a much later start in creating and developing new interests and friends apart from work. *New friends and new activities solve loneliness and can lead to meaningful relationships. Think young and act cautiously.*

Stay as healthy as you can, for as long as you can, because without good health, there's less fun in living.

Chapter 9

Where Will They Put Me?

Planning a funeral is hard enough but planning your own is one of the most frequently postponed tasks. This is especially true for couples after several marriages or relationships which involve multiple children and extended families. The arrangements for burial can become exceedingly complicated. The location of the burial plot is the most difficult question to answer and one not easily solved by your children, particularly if they do not all have the same two parents. If multiple family plots had been previously purchased during former marriages, the situation is even harder to resolve. Each family wants their parents together in their family plot. How does one ever solve this problem? We will give you an example of a friend of ours who is presently married for the third time to a woman who was previously married once before. They have no children together but each has two children from each previous marriage. That is a total of six--he has four boys and she has two girls. These six children are from three different families, none of which are intact today. When he passes on, where will they put him? Who will get him----the first family, the second family or the present wife? Other than the grim thought of burying pieces at each site, thoughtful compromise is necessary unless his wishes were made known to all of his children and his present wife prior to death. A possible solution to this dilemma, would be cremation and the distribution of the ashes to all the concerned families. It should be noted, though, that the

Jewish faith does not presently approve of cremation so this solution would not be valid if the deceased was orthodox.

We recently became aware of a couple's problem with burial location that had a happy ending for the couple but not necessarily for the children. The couple were remarried after having both been widowed, with full support from both families. They moved to Florida from their original location and established a new life for themselves. They traveled frequently, including visits to their many children. After several years they felt that their new life was full, complete and extremely happy. In making plans for their future, they decided that they wanted to be buried side by side in Florida. This drew strong objections and hurt feelings from both sides since it appeared to the children that each one was deserting their deceased parent. The couple settled the bickering by saying that this was their decision and had nothing to do with a lack of love for the deceased spouse. They hoped that all their children would be mature enough to respect their wishes and eventually they did.

Other situations can arise that cause concern and require a certain amount of deep thought. Again, these solutions should be worked out before they are needed. Here's another example. If a widow and widower marry, they should decide where they will be buried----with the first spouse or the new spouse or in a combined plot of both families. Since the remarried woman probably has a different last name now than her previous family name, the tombstone markings should include both family names to acknowledge children and grandchildren of the previous union. Although there is a cost involved, it can and should be done for the benefit of both families. If both parties agree, even if one previous spouse has been cremated, all four partners can be buried together. Most cemeteries can accommodate multiple burials in one site as long as they are aware in advance of future burial plans. Ashes can be included within the same grave site. Again, the new markings should clearly indicate both family names and the relationship of the parties so that both families can consider the site their own. Children and future grandchildren can visit both parents or grandparents in one location rather than having to visit multiple cemeteries.

Very often religious customs govern large parts of funeral arrangements and burials. Most religions have their own cemeteries but most cemeteries do not exclude people of other faiths. For example, Jewish cemeteries may have portions devoted solely to individuals of the Jewish faith but have other areas where non Jews, of any faith, can be buried. If an interfaith couple, one of whom is Jewish, want to be buried together they may do so in the interfaith section of a Jewish cemetery. Many of the rules in Jewish cemeteries are arbitrated by a Rabbi and his decision is final. Most cemeteries have sections reserved for certain faiths. Some have Catholic areas that have been blessed by a Bishop. All Protestant denominations have cemeteries where members of their congregations are buried. They are often on church grounds or in specified areas of larger cemeteries.

Couples who are unmarried usually have fewer problems since the family of the deceased makes the arrangements, including burial, with little discussion with the surviving partner. If an unmarried couple wants to be buried together, they should discuss this beforehand with both families, purchase their plot and perhaps prepay some of the expenses. It never hurts to include burial wishes in your will. How do you list the survivor of an unmarried relationship in an obituary----friend, significant other, long time companion or partner? The family may decide not to list them at all! Should the unmarried survivor participate in the wake and burial as a family member? This, again, is entirely up to the deceased's family if no prior arrangements were made. Unmarried couples are often at loose ends near a partner's time of death. Children hover and the partner is pushed aside. Even a loving family starts to think of family possessions and inheritance.

Funeral expenses are generally paid for by the family of the deceased. The surviving spouse usually pays the costs which are often covered by life insurance. If the couple are not married, and have not prepaid expenses, the costs are paid by the family or the estate of the deceased. The survivor of a long-term, unmarried couple has no legal obligation to share burial expenses but may feel they have a moral one.

Chapter 10

Dating Tips for Active Seniors

1. Don't introduce him/her to the family before the fifth date.
2. Don't talk about other relationships.
3. Try not to make weird noises or strange movements.
4. Watch your table manners.
5. Don't dwell on your family in conversation.
6. See if he/she has any special cravings (chocolate, football, cheesecake)
7. Remember nobody likes rejection but sometimes it's to your advantage down the line.
8. Do you both like card games? Can you play as partners without a quarrel?
9. Rules you learned from grandmother don't always work at this age.
10. Always remember, those that are asked out again are those that are fun to be with.
11. Place a personal ad if you like but be cautious and remember they work better for men than for women.
12. There's not enough time left to date married people.
13. Compliment him/her on the way he brought up his children.
14. Compliment him/flatter her on something small.
15. Ladies, don't join the casserole brigade. Find another way to introduce yourself.

16. Don't make the first date Dutch treat or use coupons. Let her treat you later on.
17. Treat yourself to a new "do" and an expensive outfit----you'll feel better.
18. Is he passionate about sports? If so, become interested!
19. Be a good navigator----he may learn to depend upon you.
20. Is he into Sinatra or Beethoven? Better find out.
21. Can he dance? Does he like to?
22. Don't badger him but call him sometimes.
23. If there are three women for every man----think of yourself as number one.
24. Kissing is fun but are you ready for what comes next? Don't be forced into anything but don't bank the fires if you want to stay cold.
25. Find out if he drives at night----if he doesn't----you drive.
26. Don't over organize him----he's gotten this far without you.
27. Don't ask him how much money he has----let him tell you.
28. Flowers are always nice.
29. Show her how handy you are and offer to make small repairs.
30. Instead of eating out, offer to cook her a gourmet meal.
31. Try a new men's cologne----ladies love them.
32. Don't forget the three S's----shave, shower and shine your shoes.
33. Clean out your car and give it a wash!
34. Casual doesn't mean old----take your son with you and buy something new to wear.

35. Is he a control freak? Do we need one at this age?
36. Above all, remember gifts don't need an occasion.

ABOUT THE AUTHORS

We are both in our sixties, formerly widowed and now married five years. In our new life, we have made many new friends as well as taking up golf and tennis. We travel often including visits to children living outside the country. Our family now includes seven children and ten grandchildren. Willard is a retired physician who currently teaches at the George Washington University School of Medicine and the Johns Hopkins Adult Education program. He is scheduled to teach Medical Ethics in two locations for the Elderhostel program. He is the author of a medical book as well as numerous other scientific articles.

Peggy received a degree in journalism and was a contributor to the book, *The City of Washington.* As the wife of a Foreign Service Officer, Peggy lived in several foreign countries where three out of four of her sons were born. After her husband's death, she worked for the CIA at headquarters in Langley, Virginia.

www.ingramcontent.com/pod-product-compliance
Lightning Source LLC
Chambersburg PA
CBHW020542290526
45786CB00002B/1001